NAKED LIVES

NAKED LIVES

INSIDE THE WORLDS OF EXOTIC DANCE

MINDY S. BRADLEY-ENGEN

excelsior editions

State University of New York Press
Albany, New York

Published by

State University of New York Press, Albany

© 2009 State University of New York

For information, contact State University of New York Press, Albany, NY
www.sunypress.edu

Production by Marilyn P. Semerad
Marketing by Michael Campochiaro

Library of Congress Cataloging in Publication Data

Bradley-Engen, Mindy S., 1975-
  Naked lives : inside the worlds of erotic dance / Mindy S.
Bradley-Engen.
      p. cm.
  Includes bibliographical references and index.
  ISBN 978-1-4384-2605-1 (alk. paper) — ISBN 978-1-4384-2606-8
(pbk. : alk. paper) 1. Stripteasers. 2. Stripteasers—Interviews.
3. Striptease—Social aspects. 4. Women dancers. 5. Sex in dance.
I. Title.
  PN1949.S7B73 2009
  305.9'7927—dc22

                                               2008034701

10 9 8 7 6 5 4 3 2 1

CONTENTS

ACKNOWLEDGMENTS

First, and foremost, I thank the many dancers I've met on this journey. I hope this book adequately conveys the humor, candor, and insightfulness with which these remarkable people described their experiences and shared their stories. I thank them and the club customers, staff and management (many of whom allowed me unrestricted access to their establishments) for embracing me as one of their own.

Many thanks go to the faculty and staff in the Department of Sociology and Criminal Justice at the University of Arkansas, including Anna Zajicek and Brent Smith. My wonderful colleague Lori Holyfield heard far more about exotic dance than she probably ever wanted to know, and always responded with encouragement and advice. I am also fortunate to have had the full support of my former department chair and current dean, William Schwab. His provision of resources and careful protection of my time expedited the completion of what otherwise would have been a far more arduous venture.

Several others have been extremely helpful, including John Randolph Fuller, Michael P. Johnson, Bruce Arrigo, Janet Swim, Eric Silver, Wilson Palacios, Daniel Kissinger, and Tammy Lorince. I appreciate Ron Weitzer's thoughtful reading of early drafts of this manuscript—his comments greatly improved the final product. Many thanks go to Senior Acquisitions Editor Nancy Ellegate and the good people at SUNY Press for their steady encouragement and remarkable patience in response to inexperience, confusion, and panic.

On a more personal note, I thank Stacy Seymour, who continually demonstrates the meaning of sisterhood. I am also grateful to Brent Teasdale for his love and support. A true friend, he's been right beside me at every step of this endeavor. And I thank my husband, Rod Engen. Through my best and worst moments, his love, encouragement, understanding, and protection have been unwavering. Being his partner makes life better.

Finally, I am immeasurably grateful to Jeffery T. Ulmer, my dissertation chair at Penn State University. Over the years, Jeff trained me in qualitative methods, taught me symbolic interactionism, sat through early (and horrid) presentations, helped develop ideas, read and gave feedback on numerous manuscript drafts, wrote recommendation letters, and counseled me off several personal and professional ledges. He devoted enormous amounts of time and effort to a project and a student many faculty would have never given consideration. Jeff's willingness to take risks and root for the underdog changed my life. I could not have asked for a better mentor and friend.

1

INTRODUCTION

This book draws on field observations, interviews, and my own personal experiences to expose the different social worlds of exotic dance. Rather than making judgments about stripping as a profession, saying whether or not stripping is bad for women, or merely identifying the impact of dancing on women, I investigate variation in the structural arrangement of exotic dance establishments. Throughout the following chapters, I reveal how the organization of work creates different perceptions of work. Strip clubs vary, and types of clubs contextualize the experience of exotic dancing, creating more or less circumstances in which stripping can be good, bad, or indifferent for the women involved. Portraying exotic dance establishments as distinct types of social worlds, I detail the various settings and subcultures within which exotic dancing takes place and specify how each of these contexts gives rise to its own conditions of negative affect, limitation, and obligation, as well as satisfaction and empowerment.

Working in the sex industry carries a large social stigma, of which those involved are very aware.[1] Even with the increased visibility of the sex industry in popular culture, the sex worker is generally not regarded as "normal" by others. A considerable number of federal, state, and local laws ban and/or regulate various types of sex work. The type of sex work allowed varies greatly across location, and erotic establishments are continually subject to extensive regulation. Public opinion polls report that roughly half of Americans feel that stripping should be illegal at bars or clubs (Gallup 1996). Indeed, many wonder how anyone could do this kind of work and question the character of erotic entertainers.

1

Despite, or perhaps because of, its provocative "deviant" nature, there is limited sociological research on sex work relative to other areas of inquiry. Women in the sex industry are aware of the misunderstandings and judgments associated with their work. Subsequently, sex workers may be suspicious of researchers; they may be resistant to inquiries from "outsiders." Furthermore, whereas the strip club may be sociologically fascinating for researchers, it is an occupational environment for strippers. Our research field is their job. For these women, scholarly research, theoretical debates, and sociological speculation may very well seem self-righteous, condescending, and completely irrelevant to the pragmatic issues of their daily lives. Dancers are there to work; they may really not want to be bothered by some academic "tourists."

Furthermore, regardless of numerous books and high-quality articles (mostly in specialty journals), it seems sex work has yet to gain its rightful legitimacy in social science. Those who pursue this line of research may find getting grants or publishing in mainstream academic journals is an even tougher task compared to many of their non–sex work colleagues (regardless of the quality of their work). I recently experienced having an editor of a well-ranked mainstream journal describe my work as "T and A." He overruled the recommendations for publication made by all of the reviewers and rejected the manuscript solely on its "inappropriate" topic. I suspect this type of rejection, and my subsequent frustration and disheartenment, is not unique. Undoubtedly, some sociologists, possibly out of fear of the stigma associated with being labeled a "sex researcher," and the corresponding career obstacles, have avoided or eventually abandoned research interests in this area. This is unfortunate; as a consequence, the structure of the sex industry, the organization of sex work, and the social influences on sex workers' lives remain underexplored relative to other social phenomena.

Recognizing the deficiency in sociological discourse in her recent presidential address to the Midwest Sociological Society, Joane Nagel urged "sociologists to consider sexuality and the role of sexual systems in their own research" (2000, 1). Similarly, recent scholars have stressed the need for more research specifically on sex work (Weitzer 2000a, 2000b; Lerum 1998). Such research is essential for understanding the opportunities and obstacles sex workers encounter, including the organizational and political influences within the sex industry and making informed decisions regarding relevant legal and social policies.

As a sociologist and former sex worker, I regularly speak to classes and groups about my experiences and research. Many people are intrigued by the sex industry and want to understand how it works. But they also share larger concerns: Is stripping bad for women? Should you feel guilty about going to a strip club? Beyond the sheer fascination with the sex industry, most want to know if they are "hurting" women by patronizing these establishments—if the women who work there have been abused and are being exploited. Are these clubs dens of sin and broken dreams, filled with downtrodden women, selling their bodies out of desperation? Or are these women strong and sexually liberated, making viable career choices? By visiting these establishments, are you degrading women, or are you appreciating the female body? Such questions I regularly encounter, in various forms.

This book is a step toward answering these and similar questions. In short, the quick answers to all of these questions are, sometimes yes, sometimes no, and sometimes yes and no. Yes, sometimes, the strip club is degrading and exploitive. But at times it is not. Exotic dancing is complex and can include a number of diverse and even contradictory experiences. So, yes, on some occasions you should feel bad about going to a strip club. But sometimes you should not. You should go and hand your money over enthusiastically and enjoy yourself, unashamed. And then there are situations that are more ambiguous. Often, you hand over your money, and both you and the strippers have some mixed feelings about the whole situation. *But by all means you should hand over your money.* Now that you have the brief and no doubt unsatisfying answers, in the rest of the book I will try to explain these answers as thoroughly as possible.

Many who study sex work care deeply about this topic and are greatly concerned with the lives of sexually stigmatized groups. As previously noted, to be a sex work researcher, one has to be passionate about the subject matter. As academic rebels, we should respect our tenacity and celebrate our passion, yet be careful to avoid trading empiricism for sententiousness. Polemical advocacy compromises academic rigor. I am concerned when encountering works that initiate research based on the position that sex work is degrading. The authors conduct research that, not surprisingly, reinforces the view that this work is injurious and speculates as to the various negative consequences of erotic labor.

Interestingly, through my work as a dancer, I quickly learned that dancers themselves are aware of the larger "victims-versus-agents" controversy and use it to their advantage. Strippers, by trade, tell customers what they want to hear. And, based on my own experiences as well as those of fellow dancers, I know that the victim-versus-agency debate is alive and well in the strip club. Dancers draw on this debate regularly when interacting with customers to make money. Indeed, they are aware that people are questioning whether dancers are women down on their luck. They make the most of this guilt and stereotype to increase tips. More than once have I observed dancers playing the "sympathy card" with their regulars, describing how they are in desperate need of cash for their children or rent. This is a valuable money-making tactic, often used independent of actual need. Making men feel sorry for them, dancers often play on a client's desire to "save" them. It is a common practice to play on the victim status to manipulate clients into giving dancers extra money or paying bills. I have done it myself and can verify that it is extremely profitable.

Whereas some customers are best manipulated by the sympathy card, others find this to be a turnoff. Guilt can be effective for some clients but not for others. If they feel guilty about being at a club, they may not stay very long. If they see the strip club as full of downtrodden, desperate women, they may feel shameful and leave. This can substantially impact dancers' tips. In order to avoid "scaring them off," dancers may try to portray themselves as happy and content with their jobs; the upbeat attitude of the sex worker makes people feel more comfortable about patronizing these establishments. Thus, they try to portray themselves as "party girls" who are just young and having fun. This "agent" status relieves customers' sense of guilt about patronizing strip clubs. When patrons are having fun, they spend money. I learned this early on and quickly became a master of the artificial good time.

Social science has yet to adequately take these skills into account when interviewing dancers or other sexual performers. In these occupations, telling people what they want to hear becomes common practice, if not a job requirement. If a dancer believes a customer needs to feel better about her employment, she will portray herself as empowered. In contrast, if she has a customer who feels sorry for her, she will use that to her advantage as well. In other words, dancers play out the gendered understandings of the occupation in interactions. This is a talent; dancers are accustomed to reading subtle cues to decide how to portray themselves, especially with regard to the victims-versus-agency issue. Indeed, it is not surprising that sociological works written by former sex workers often find dancers espousing the liberties of dancing, whereas works by advocates or critics of sex work find sex work to be degrading.

For example, in her recent work, *Stripped*, Barton (2006) comments on current research's lack of insight from former sex workers and questions whether her study should include participant observation. She concludes that she could not bring herself to be a participant, and thus does not overcome the same shortcoming she laments. Specifically, she describes her decision not to dance: "I soon discovered that simply watching the show swiftly drained most of my emotional reserves. In the beginning, I felt depressed and exhausted after only forty-five minutes in a club. After a few months of visiting the bars and getting to know some of the dancers, I learned to tolerate the noise, the smoke, and the undiluted testosterone for about one to two hours before I had the irresistible impulse to leave at once. Clearly dancing was not an option for me . . . I quickly grasped that the role of a *sympathetic outsider* would more easily facilitate researching this book" (2006, 4–5, emphasis added).

The sympathetic outsider? Upon reading this, I knew immediately that the subsequent findings would reinforce the researcher's perception of dancers as exploited and characterizations of male customers as "undiluted testosterone." Taking this position, Barton then proceeds to conclude that dancing is emotionally draining and oppressive. However, it is reasonable to suspect that, despite attempts to conceal her negative feelings, dancers may have perceived her distaste for stripping and her sympathy for the women who do it. Her work thus demonstrates the difficulties of interviewing exotic dancers and how these interviews can be easily led by the interviewer ideology.

My own experience with dancers renders her conclusions seriously questionable. In her book, Barton talks openly about her refusal to dance, her revulsion at the idea of dancing, and her pity for dancers. I was thus "underwhelmed" by the conclusion that dancing has long-term negative consequences for women and by her characterization that it is only satisfying to the extent to which

women's performances conform to the clients' gendered expectations. These results did not ring of unbiased empiricism and thus
were neither particularly surprising nor compelling. It is possible
that, based upon subtle and inadvertent social and conversational
cues, the dancers she interviewed quickly identified a potential
bias, determined what she wanted to hear about the "toll" of
stripping, and gave her answers to establish that finding. They
quickly sized up the situation and went into misfortune mode.
This may be particularly true if she entered the field in a customer-
like role and/or was giving dancers money (this seems to be the
case, based on her description). How is this possibility for
response bias taken into account?

Some may say that the act of stripping is degrading in any
context; that is, it is demeaning for women in any club, by reducing them to physical bodies.[2] To say that stripping in itself is
degrading based solely on the fact that attention is being placed on
nudity and sexuality naked assumes that being looked at as a
physical body is inherently degrading. Humans are physical
beings; being seen physically and sexually does not in itself dehu-
manize. Being looked at as a physical being, noticed for one's
physical attributes, is only demeaning if it is unwanted. If one does
not want to be looked at as purely a physical or sexual being, then
stripping can be demeaning. But this may be the case in any occupation. A teacher or lawyer who is seen as a sexual object rather
than a colleague is being degraded. But what if one does want to
be seen in such a manner or really does not mind? Perhaps it is
somehow inherently wrong, and people who want to be seen as
sex objects are misguided (though I seriously doubt that). But that
does not change the fact that they do want to be seen that way,
and many really do not feel bad about it.

Is it not reasonable that at least some women may want, in
some particular instances, to be seen only as sexual creatures? On
occasion, some women (or men for that matter) may want to be
seen as sex objects. A beautiful woman may want to be seen and
admired for her appearance; she may find praise for her physical
attributes satisfying. She may desire to be seen sexually. The idea
that, on occasion, women and men may want to be sexualized in
some circumstances is certainly not new. Exotic dancers are not
the only individuals who are rewarded for and seek prize for their
physical attributes. Let's not kid ourselves. Strippers did not invent
tanning beds, breast augmentation, sexy outfits, high heels, or lin-

gerie. They just brought them all together in one place and made money off of them.

There is reason to believe that, because it is based on its portrayal and exaggeration of gender roles and the commodification of women, sex work, such as prostitution and exotic dance, is a reproduction of larger gender inequality. Such arguments are often found within the genre of feminist literature (for some examples, see the works of MacKinnon 1989; MacKinnon and Dworkin 1998; Farley 2004; Raphael and Shapiro 2004; Raymond 1995, 1998). These arguments may have merit for larger social issues, but I believe this is missing the point. While it may very well be that larger gender inequality creates the market and labor that guarantee continued existence of sex work, that does not mean that being a sex worker is inherently wholly detrimental for women. In other words, while it may be that gender inequality produces the conditions that allow there to be a sex work industry, this does not mean that the women who participate in it are not making choices. Within these larger social constraints, women do have some agency. Let us not cast them all as weak, hopeless sufferers; to do so belittles them. By all means, if you feel bad going to a strip club, then do not go. But I seriously doubt that the closing of strip clubs would bring about an end to larger social inequality.

One may say (and many have said) that a dancer may enjoy her work, yet, at some assumed higher level of abstraction (apparently beyond her own understanding), she nevertheless is being exploited. Thus, we cannot assume a women is not being exploited because she willingly participates in her degradation. Perhaps this is so. This begs the question: If not the women involved, who is to decide whether or not something is degrading *to them*? Researchers, perhaps? Advocates? Scholars?

The idea that "we" determine that "they" are being exploited, even if their own comments imply that they are not, is condescending and runs the risk of ignoring our data. This position suggests that somehow we recognize their experience better than they do. It allows us to simply dismiss any evidence that contradicts our premise. We know what we want to find and will cast aside any contradictory response as false consciousness. By dismissing their interpretations of their own situations, we are, although perhaps not intentionally, saying they are not aware enough or intelligent enough to make sense of their surroundings. That position

certainly seems to demean these women and their own sense of
themselves and their lives. Gender inequality exists, but it does not
mean women are not strong, resilient, and independent. To con-
demn sex work as degradation and dismiss the variation in the
erotic laborers' understanding of their world undermines many
women's sense of agency and belittles their choices—often all in the
name of "helping" them. Some authors claim to be "giving these
women a voice" but then discard what they do not like to hear.

Alternatively, works written by many proud current and
former sex workers dispute the findings of anti–sex work scholars.
These writings must be interpreted with caution as well. My own
research findings, among others, suggest that there are indeed
women who choose this profession and take pride in this work
(Bradley 2007). While their firsthand experiences suggest sex
work can be fulfilling and a source of satisfaction, the reader must
be aware that they may not be representative of the population of
dancers. Many of these authors acknowledge that their status as
authors and/or scholars suggests that they may be particularly
advantaged relative to the typical dancer. There are lots of strippers. I suspect a select few write their own books. I doubt whether
their experiences are the same as the many women who probably
will not become professors, authors, journalists, or independently
wealthy. That does not mean that even relatively privileged
women involved in sexual labor do not face many potentially
degrading or exploitive encounters. Many of these works describe
traumatizing experiences along with stories of empowerment and
self-acceptance.

Perhaps my own approach has created new dilemmas. It is not
my intention to berate the work of any researchers. Rather, I hope
that my work will complement the fine work of my fellow
researchers. Social phenomena are best informed by multiple perspectives. My goal here is to build on these works, putting the
autobiographical works of dancers in context and highlighting the
potential benefits of placing the social scientific findings in context.

Throughout this book, I operationalize degradation based on
more concrete definitions of situations. In other words, I suggest
that stripping, and sex work more generally, is degrading *if the
women involved in it feel degraded*. It is exploitive if the women
do not enjoy their work, do not want to be there, and feel compelled to do it. And yes, I find that sometimes they do feel that
way. Other times they do not. Other times, they feel a sense of

agency in their work; they choose to work in these jobs, choose these jobs over viable alternatives, and find satisfaction in their careers; they like what they do. And many times they may have mixed feelings about their jobs, characterizing their work as a mixture of agentic and oppressive moments. My purpose here is to contextualize the work of stripping as it relates to dancer perceptions of their work. If the argument is that stripping is degrading for the women who work in the profession, then we must explore potential variations in their subjective experiences, as well as in possible correlates of their experiences.

In this book I try to give the reader an understanding of the negative, positive, and ambivalent characterizations of stripping *as these women understand it*. To do so requires that I do not take on what I believe to be the larger question of personal beliefs. I must describe what I hear and observe and look for systematic themes and correlates across individual experiences. My own life may be insightful and provide clues and suggestions for inquiry; but I must not cloud the data with prejudgments or make larger ideological implications that go beyond the scope of my data and analyses. To take the position that sex work is systematically bad is to impose one's own morality on an entire occupation, independent of the varying opinions of those involved in this line of work. And, to be sure, how I feel about the profession in general is less important than how sex workers themselves experience their work.

MY INTEREST

In *The Conceptual Practices of Power: A Feminist Sociology of Knowledge* (1991), Dorothy Smith describes her difficulty in separating her personal feelings and values as a woman and her scholarly work as a sociologist and researcher. That is, in an effort to define her work as value neutral and academic, she attempted to remove herself from her work. In her feminist critiques of sociology, she states that too often scholars are trained to disregard their own personal experiences as a source of reliable information about the character of the world. She concludes that it is an impossibility. Smith argues that the only way of knowing a socially constructed world is by knowing it from within. Not only is it false to believe that researchers can avoid being human in their research, but belief in strict objectivity ignores the valuable insight and genuineness that comes from being an insider (Smith 1991, 1989).

This spirit of identifying with one's life experiences and allowing them to motivate and guide one's research agenda is critical for the production of sociological knowledge. Smith concludes, "I am not proposing an immediate and radical transformation of the methods of the discipline . . . What I am suggesting is more in the nature of reorganizing the relationship of sociologist to the object of our knowledge . . . This involves first placing sociologists where we are actually situated . . . making our direct embodied experience of the everyday world the primary ground of our knowledge" (1991, 377).

Consistent with this perspective, researchers in the study of deviance have regularly integrated their life experiences with their sociological training to produce highly regarded ethnographic research. For example, Becker's research on the lives of jazz musicians and the lives of outsiders originates in his own experiences as a jazz musician (1963). More recently, Elijah Anderson (2003) wrote about his entrée into African American corner and liquor store culture, which led to the influential *Code of the Street: Decency, Violence, and the Moral Life of the Inner City* (1999). Describing his research at Jelly's place, a street corner tavern setting, Anderson found that his own experience drove his inquiry into this area of research. He believed that "one of the main reasons I may have gravitated to this setting was that it gave me the opportunity to think about my own background, my own story, even important aspects of my identity" (2003, 217).

In this tradition, the current ethnographic study began as an autobiographical venture undertaken during my career in exotic dance. Specifically, I set out to understand why I made the choices I made, danced when, where, and how I did, and, above all, had so much difficulty terminating my career as a dancer. Much like Anderson, I became increasingly aware of the tension I experienced throughout my dance and graduate career; a tension "based on the awareness that I lived in two worlds" (Anderson 2003, 235).

Experiencing this duality, being at once in the social world of the university where I was an overworked graduate student of questionable ability and, simultaneously, a highly regarded and successful dancer in the world of adult entertainment highlighted both the similarities and the differences of each social world. Both worlds had moments of satisfaction and uncertainty. There were moments when I was simultaneously proud of my ability as a dancer and ashamed of my performance as a student. On Friday night I was a goddess, and on Monday morning I was entirely unremarkable. But there were also times that I thanked God I was in graduate school and not "just a dancer." My pride in producing a good paper or performing well on an exam fell on deaf ears at the strip club. I became well aware of the organization and expectations of these distinct social worlds. I began journaling my experiences, thinking that perhaps these notes would help me understand my own ambivalence.

During this time, I began reading works written by other sex workers, specifically exotic dancers. Authors such as Heidi Mattson, Lily Burana, and Cheryl Bartlett described the trials and tribulations of sexual labor.[3] Their stories do not glorify stripping but reveal all the complex experiences of dancing. Yet, for all the negative experiences, these women chose to pursue this line of work. In fact, these women, and many other such authors, found it incredibly difficult to quit working in the sex industry. The image of dancers portrayed in these works counters popular perceptions of sex workers as dumb, unskilled, or abused (Sweet and Tewksbury 2003; Ronai and Ellis 1989; Prus and Irini 1980; Salutin 1971).

These women were bright, articulate, and educated. They had choices; they were not desperate, poor, or without agency or options. Mattson continued to work as a dancer, long after graduating from Brown University. Similarly, Burana, journalist and former stripper, reentered dancing shortly after getting engaged. She felt compelled, for reasons she herself does not fully comprehend, to dance one more year. She was satisfied in her life and relationships yet undertook a farewell journey stripping at clubs across the country. Her trip was one of self-understanding and life transition, not one of desperation or exploitation. Bartlett, shortly after receiving her Ph.D. and taking a new job, began moonlighting as a dancer. She explains her entry in dance as driven by her desire to know and experience her body, to be physical, and to take control of her life. "Having always been a person more cerebral than physical, I tend to live a pleasant, if sedentary life firmly stationed in my mind . . . When I turned thirty, along with the extra weight, my hormones went crazy. I began to feel not just more sexual, but sensual. I have a new confidence in my body that

I couldn't have even imagined before, and now I revel in it. I would hate to waste this feeling" (2003, 15–16).[4]

Their stories seemed remarkably similar to my own. Originating in my own lived experience, my interest in this topic as academic research emerged from my formal training in the sociology of deviance and social psychology. From this training, I became interested in getting to know and understand the experiences of other dancers; I began to see this area as a sociological phenomenon. My original intention was to understand my own motivations. However, my interactions with other dancers and sociological training suggested that my experiences were not atypical.

I strongly identified with these authors and their stories and longed to understand this work as a sociological experience. Much of the current sociological literature has focused on the research questions related to the actual process of performing sexual labor: what these women do, how they talk to clients, client motivations, the role of the bouncer. That is, work on strippers and by strippers has revealed much about the techniques and experiences of exotic dancers and other strip club actors. In their well-known study on stripping, Ronai and Ellis (1989) described the tactics utilized by dancers in their interactions with customers. They reveal how dancers use speech and body language in their work, often feigning interest, flirting, or pretending to be what they perceive a specific customer finds appealing. Such strategies as the use of particular costumes, conversational tactics, and so on, are readily employed by dancers to make them more attractive to customers and to increase customer spending. Enck and Preston's (1988) dramaturgical analysis of exotic dancing revealed similar findings.

In addition to interactions with customers, studies have also examined dancer strategies in negotiations with management and the stresses associated with working conditions. Recent work by Egan (2006) explores the tactical use of music in dancer-customer and dancer-management interactions. She found that music is often used by dancers as a form of covert protest. When dancers have difficulties with customers or with management they often select music with lyrics that express their hostility. Moreover, playing "their music" becomes a statement of independence and a coping mechanism for dealing with aversive working conditions. Other research has explored similar topics such as background characteristics (Sweet and Tewksbury 2003), management pressures for body modification (Wesely 2003a), or dancer strategies for adjusting to the conditions associated with exotic dancing (Sweet and Tewksbury 2000; Wesely 2003b; Barton 2002; Deshotels and Forsyth 2006; Bradley 2008).

Although not explicitly the focus, numerous studies provide evidence of differences in club structure. Earlier research on exotic dancing, such as early research by McCaghy and Skipper (1972) and Boles and Garbin (1974), acknowledged dancer preferences across clubs yet did not make distinct club-level organizational comparisons. More recently, in her (2002) analysis on male motivations for patronizing exotic dance establishments, Frank discusses her experiences across clubs with regard to dress codes, tipping policies, and other social practices. Differences in recruitment and retention practices have been documented among friendship networks in brothels as well as erotic clubs (Chapkis 1997).

Furthermore, research by Sweet and Tewksbury (2000) reveals substantial differences between what motivates strippers to continue working. They posited three ideal types of strippers in terms of their motivation to continue their dancing career: (1) the career dancer, who continued to work to make money, (2) the party dancer, whose lifestyle centered on consumption of drugs and alcohol, and (3) the power dancer, who obtained rewards through the act of being desired by others. This typology of dancer revealed that there is variation in the experience and motivation of dancers. However, these authors do not investigate possible social organizational variations that might produce these dancer types.

Moreover, structural variation in the "image" promoted by organizations may influence individual sex worker motivations and experiences. For example, Skipper and McCaghy (1970, 1971), in a study of strippers, found that dancers at some clubs were more likely to report that their role as a dancer was "entertaining." These dancers were also more likely than others to report using dancing to gain entry into more glamorous professions, such as professional dancing, acting, or modeling.

I have opted to examine the contextual variations that underlie much of the literature and unpack their meaning. In researching this book, I have taken a number of roles, both participating and relatively unobtrusive. This book draws on my many different approaches to studying stripping, including participant observation as a dancer, dressing room assistant, and barmaid, as well as unobtrusive field observations, dressing room interviews, and outside interviews. This diversity of data collection perspectives allows me to give a vivid description of the larger culture and organization in which dancers experience their work.

While there are certainly individual personalities and differences that dancers bring to their jobs, part (I believe a great deal) of how dancers understand and feel about their vocation is conditioned by the organizations in which they work. I have tried to draw upon my own personal lived experience for insight yet maintain the sociological distance requisite in my role as a researcher. Some of my experiences are included to add illustrative depth to my analyses. But this is not my autobiography; rather, I use some of my own story as a framework to help the reader understand the social worlds of dance and the varied experiences of exotic dancers.

Furthermore, I develop a theoretical explanation for how variation in these situational interactions can have substantial effects on perceptions of career agency and constraint. I conclude by arguing that the organization of sex work creates the conditions under which dancers feel internally and/or externally motivated and experience agency or constraint. I present a typology of club organizations, including the hustle, social, and show clubs, and discuss how the conditions of work vary across these clubs. I then discuss how the unique contextual features of each club lead to variations in career commitment development.

APPLYING A SOCIAL WORLDS PERSPECTIVE

Many scholars have argued against the one-dimensional understandings of sex workers' lives as exploitation or agency (Egan and Frank 2005; Barton 2002; Weitzer 2000a, 2005a, 2005b). I wholeheartedly agree. Throughout the following chapters, I detail not only how dancers experience their work but the larger cultural influence in which these dancers' perceptions take shape. In doing so, the current study is consistent with the social-worlds/processual-order perspective developed by Anselm Strauss and his colleagues (Strauss et al., 1963; Strauss 1984, 1993).[5]

The processual-order approach stresses interactions between identities and organizational context. This perspective focuses on the reciprocity between higher-level conditions and individual actions. Within a society there are a multitude of networks of regular activity and mutual response. These *social worlds* are defined by lines of communication and participation and encompass various subworlds, subcomponents segmented by allegiances, access to resources, professional identities, ideology, and so on. Thus, individual-level phenomena cannot be understood independent of the large structures in which they exist, and, in turn, larger social organizations cannot be understood without an appreciation of human interpersonal behavior (Strauss et al. 1963; Strauss 1984, 1993).[6]

Larger social structures create situations in which people act, and, in turn, people's actions can change, modify, or reinforce the larger social structure. So, applying a social-worlds perspective entails taking into account interaction processes as well as structural features within which individuals act. Thus, I detail the organizational culture and informal structure in which members of the exotic dance environment do "sex work." That is, in the strip club, the product is continually created as members individually interpret experiences within a social context.

The framework I put forth is for conceptual clarity, not to be used to dichotomize women's experience. Rather, I conceptualize this club schema as a continuum of social worlds. Although the majority of clubs fall into a particular category, the strip club typology presented is not intended to be discrete classification schema. In other words, although each type is presented separately for conceptual clarity, this typology represents a *continuum* of club organizational patterns. That is, not all clubs can be uniquely classified as one distinct "hustle," "social," or "show" club. Rather, I suggest that clubs will exhibit patterns of dancer perceptions and commitment development similar to those outlined in this study to the extent that a particular club displays organizational features that characterize a certain type.

This book does not necessarily contradict accusations of sex work, nor does it confirm them. I believe that my role as a sociologist is to understand social phenomena as an individual's lived reality. My job is to reflect people's commonsense understanding of their lived experience of social life. In this tradition, I posit that a thorough understanding of sex work is best informed by looking at the profession through the eyes of those who do it.

2

METHODOLOGY

This book draws on more than eight years of experience in strip clubs. The findings presented here stem from three years of participant observation as a dancer in at least thirty-seven clubs; two years of participant observation as a waitress, customer, and third party backstage and in dressing rooms in at least twelve clubs; and another three years of observation at numerous clubs throughout the continental United States. This book also includes information from fifty formal interviews with dancers, roughly twelve hours of recorded dressing room conversations, two phone interviews, and three e-mail interviews.

I began working as an exotic dancer in 1999. Soon after I began dancing, "my club" (which was the only club in town) closed for remodeling. In the interim, I began shopping for another club to call home. I danced a night here or there, to see what establishment was both lucrative and within reasonable driving distance.

I quickly learned that the experience of dancing was highly varied. Sometimes I hated it. Sometimes I came home and scrubbed my entire body. I just felt awful. I had heard disgusting things, been spoken to like I was worthless and stupid, and I took it. With every inappropriate touch, every greasy and presumptuous probing finger or overt tongue, my inner angry feminist raged. Yet I tolerated these things and felt enormous anger at myself for allowing these events to happen to me. I swore I would never go back to the club, and had tremendous respect for the women who did.

Why did women continue to dance when they had awful experiences? I soon learned that these women felt compelled to be there.

They had few choices for earning as much money as quickly. Frankly, dancing was perceived to be the only viable option, no matter how much they did not enjoy the actual working experience. They felt "stuck." Although many women expressed concern over their ability to meet the demands of conventional employment, the proportion of women who reported being drug and/or alcohol dependent varied significantly across clubs. Others consistently reported that they felt forced to remain in exotic dance because it offered them an opportunity for fast money and flexible hours to accommodate childcare concerns. The following quote demonstrates how many exotic dancers feel compelled to continue dancing in order to meet financial and family demands: "I'm a single mother of three. Their father doesn't give me a dime. But at least he's involved in their lives. If I take him to court, he might not stay like that. So I take care of my kids. I do the best I can" (Mercy, thirty-one, danced for more than ten years).

Stories like this make dancing seem like a desperate option. But this is not always the case. Yes, I had some of those horrible experiences (and I will share some of them). But sometimes I loved it (and I will share some of those stories too). Sometimes I had so much fun I wished I could quit my "real job" and just keep dancing. I was a goddess. I was fun and flirtatious. I drank for free and heard how beautiful I was all night. I was erotic and powerful. I felt connected with my body. I moved and swayed and sang along with my favorite music. I was beautiful and comfortable in my own skin, unapologetic. I came home, looked at myself in the mirror, and experienced the kind of total acceptance and appreciation that virtually never occurs in contemporary society. I was proud of my body and sexuality.

So did I find dancing to be degrading or empowering? I found both. Moreover, I found that my own experiences were not unique. And yes, while in any work environment one can have both positive and negative experiences, I found consistent patterns that increase the likelihood of feeling particular types of constraint or agency across clubs. Although all clubs sold sex, *how* they sold sex was very different, and these differences worked to create varying experiences of agency and constraint. In other words, similarities and differences in the organization of clubs impacted the day-to-day experiences of dancers.

This suggested that dancers negotiate their identities based on structural contexts of clubs. Because the contexts of individual clubs varied, the definition of dancer identity and corresponding dancer roles varied. Subsequently, clubs varied on their ability to attract and retain different types of dancers. In addition, dancers within a particular type of club socialized new members into the culture of that club to effectively maintain these subcultural distinctions. For some women the experience of dancing appeared to be positive, whereas for others dancing was experienced negatively. That is, there were significant differences across dancers in terms of what it means to be a dancer, and, moreover, these differences appeared to be related to the locations in which these women performed their work. What it means to be a dancer as an individual varied across dancers in accordance with what it means to be a dancer generically in a particular club.

· During this time, I began working with Jeffery Ulmer, my graduate school mentor. I had been recording my feelings and observations for some time, thinking that one day in my distant future I would look back on my notes and reminisce. I knew my observations and experiences had sociological merit but did not think any advisor would knowingly sign on to such a controversial topic. I was wonderfully wrong. With his encouragement, I soon resolved not only to undertake my first qualitative research project but also to make it my dissertation. I began studying qualitative methodology and set out to dance and work in as many different places as possible.

Not knowing what direction my research would take, I recorded as much information about each of these locations as I could, often in exhaustive detail. I regularly took field notes regarding the club policies; the clientele, dancer, and staff characteristics; money-earning strategies of clubs and dancers; and dancer interactions. I continued to journal my own experiences, feelings, and thoughts as well. At the end of each week, I reviewed these notes with Jeff. He patiently endured the many interruptions to his own work, guided me to additional literature, and made invaluable suggestions. Through our conversations, I was able to organize my thoughts, add even more detail, and identify emerging themes.

By the end of my dance career in 2002, I had collected participant observational data and semistructured, open-ended interviews with strip club participants from thirty-seven clubs, ranging from go-go clubs (in which the dancers wore pasties to conceal their nipples and panties to cover their genitals) to fully nude establishments. I had danced in clubs throughout the southern, midwestern, and northeastern United States.

Later, from 2002 onward, with the consent of club management, I engaged in purely observational research in twelve additional establishments, both as a customer and, by drawing on my ties as a former dancer, as a neutral subject, spending time with dancers backstage and in dressing rooms. In addition to purely observational research, I occasionally worked as a barmaid or dressing room attendant. During this time, as an effort to integrate my own insights with the experiences of others, I consciously reentered the strip club environment as a field researcher. I utilized my preexisting relationships with dancers and club staff to gain entry into the research fields. Having been employed throughout these locations enabled me to rely on friendships and acquaintanceships to establish rapport with other dancers and staff so as to facilitate interviews. My initial interviews consisted primarily of open-ended questions and conversational dialogue.[1] I knew that I wanted to study women doing sex work, and I knew that it was a location ripe with sociology "in action," so I simply allowed my observations to guide me.

I took field notes regarding the various physical layouts of the clubs, the different organizational structures, the different work strategies, and the interpersonal interactions of the dancers and club owners. At the end of every observation period (ranging from three to fourteen hours), I reviewed these notes and revised them to provide more thorough detail. Occasionally, with the consent of dancers, I tape-recorded dressing room conversations. Recordings included conversations in which I was present but did not participate, as well as conversations in which I was involved. This resulted in a total of approximately twelve hours of recorded conversations. These tapes were later transcribed and coded for analysis. Two additional phone and three e-mail interviews were conducted with dancers and club owners in two western states and one midwestern state.

In addition to my own dance career, since fall 2002, I spent (and continue to spend) all my available time with strippers and in strip clubs. I relied on what I saw and heard to access the thoughts and behavioral strategies of exotic dancers and structural features of exotic dance establishments. I have traveled extensively, seeking out clubs throughout the United States. I spoke to dancers, bartenders, managers, deejays, bouncers, customers, and others in order to understand the day-to-day operations of strip clubs and what experiences women have working there.

What does one do while "hanging out" in a strip club? In addition to recording my own perceptions and detailed field notes in a journal, I conducted both private and field interviews with several dancers, customers, and club owners. With the consent of club management, I also engaged in purely observational research of variations in club physical and organizational structure, work strategies, and interpersonal interactions.

At first, being a female nonemployee in a strip club was awkward, for me as well as for the dancers and clients whom I encountered. Quite frankly, women wondered what the heck I was doing there, and, more important, if I was going to compete for their money. It may have been my "research site," but it was their job, and I was never allowed to forget that. To counter this, I took on a variety of jobs or tasks that would assist me in "blending in," often helping out as a cocktail waitress or deejay. Having a purpose for being there made my presence innocuous. Ultimately, I spent the bulk of my time backstage or in dressing rooms. These locations allowed me to talk with dancers candidly, in that they did not have to worry about how their remarks might be perceived by management and clientele. Most often, dancers who entered the dressing room would ask me why I was there. I told them I was a student, studying dancers and strip clubs, and that I was not there to "work" (dance) and would stay out of the way. This answer seemed sufficient; most women quickly got over their initial reservations and became very candid in their discussions with each other, as well as with me.

I spoke with everyone and anyone who was willing to talk with me, in any manner in which they were willing to communicate (phone, e-mail, in-person, etc.). Due to the difficulty in accessibility of the population, participants were recruited on a voluntary basis through verbal/e-mail request for participation. In addition to interviewing those already identified as meeting the criteria for inclusion, I asked participants to refer me to other individuals who might also be willing to participate. All potential interviewees were notified of the nature of study and assured of confidentiality.

Over the years, I participated in a number of activities with both staff and dancers. Occasionally, I was a participant only. During these times, I focused on being "in the moment," trying to immerse myself in the research site and absorb as much of the environment as possible. I participated in conversations both within and outside the club environment, went to dinners, parties, and nightclubs, and washed cars at a charity fundraiser sponsored by a strip club. I was present at a two-day motorcycle run celebrating the fifteen-year anniversary of one club and the annual picnic of another. At the end of these evenings, I recorded my own thoughts, feelings, and experiences.

My routine attendance established me as a "regular" in many clubs. My presence in several clubs became commonplace, and, as such, inconspicuous. I had gotten to know many dancers through previous or current employment in other clubs. This familiarity helped me gain access to new locations.

ANALYTICAL APPROACH

My approach to data collection and analysis is rooted in grounded theory methodology. Drawing on the traditions of each of its founders, Barney G. Glaser and Anselm L. Strauss, grounded theory methodology combines the rigorous quantitative approach associated with Columbia University with the rich qualitative sociological traditions of the Chicago School (Glaser and Strauss 1967; Strauss and Corbin 1990). The result is an empirical approach that aims at developing inductively derived theoretical explanations of social phenomena. Consistent with this approach, my data analysis and data collection occurred simultaneously. That is, although they are presented separately for clarification, in grounded theory, methodology data collection and analyses are joint acts.

The grounded theory approach employs a constant comparative method; this method involves systematic comparison of incidents applicable to particular categories and the integration of categories. First, I delineated the structural features of each club. As I entered each establishment, I took note of each contextual element, such as the population size of dancers and clients, the number of dancers on stage at a time, the number of interactions between management and dancers, the amount of touching, the types of policies in place. From the open coding of initial interviews and observation, a number of emergent concepts developed. Common themes surrounding the way in which work gets done, the way dancers feel about doing their work, and their reasons for being there emerged. The selection of these core categories led to the development of more focused interviews and coding schema.

After coding a number of clubs, I noticed that particular traits grouped together—that is, some contextual features seemed to co-occur. Certain club characteristics clustered together. For example, I noticed that clubs with a large number of dancers often had few interactions between dancers. Although these groupings were not perfect, general patterns of coexisting club properties emerged (for clarification, see the sample coding scheme in figure 2.1). By loosely grouping these traits together, I was able to identity three relatively distinct patterns of club organization. In other words, out of this coding schema, the latent concept of three-fold club typology emerged. After developing this typology, I utilized it to categorize future clubs during subsequent data collection.

My next step was to outline the cultural definitions and approaches to work associated with each type of club. I identified properties surrounding the phenomenon of stripteasing. These properties, such as the sexual emphasis, the financial exchange, and the physical location, were each categorized along several dimensions. For example, I rated interactions regarding the property of financial exchange along the dimension of the extent of reward during the financial exchange, the visibility of the exchange, and the amount of autonomy during the financial exchange. During each interaction I observed or in which I participated, I asked myself, "What is going on here?" I looked at each characteristic of the interactions, including the context in which they occurred, and the overall objectives of each party involved.

I then rated the relationship between resultant categories, delimiting and writing theory. This process occurred repeatedly, with each stage remaining into the next stage. After every night of observation or interview, I came home, typed up all details, and began ordering them—putting ideas together, taking them apart, and creating stacks. Throughout this time I kept diligent notes and recorded my conversations and observations on the work and lives of the dancers, focusing on their interactions with each other, customers, and club management.

While coding data in a particular category, I evaluated prior incidents in the same category or different groups in the same category. I compared events across different types of club structure as well as negotiation strategies frequently employed. This research

FIGURE 2.1. ABBREVIATED SAMPLE OF OPEN CODING CLUB CLASSIFICATION

Club Classification Schema

Club Characteristics	Hustle											Social												Show														
	a	b	c	d	e'	f	g	h	i	j	k	a	b	c	d	e	f	g	h	i	j**	k	l	a	b	c	d	e	f	g	h	i	j	k	l	m	n**	o
High Dancer Turnover	X	X	X	X	X	X	X	X	X	X	X															X											X	X	X
Assymetrical Power Relations	X	X	X	X	X	X	X	X	X	X	X															X											X	X	
Aggressive Sales	X	X	X	X	X	X	X	X	X	X	X			X												X											X		
Emphasis on Sex	X	X	X	X	X	X	X	X	X	X	X	X																									X	X	
Stage Fees	X	X	X	X	X	X	X	X	X	X	X													X													X	X	
Multiple Dancers Frequently on Stage	X	X	X	X	X	X	X	X	X	X	X																										X		X
Nonenforcement of Club Policies	X	X	X	X	X	X	X	X	X	X	X				X									X	X												X	X	
High Money Making Potential	X						X	X	X	X	X					X								X	X												X	X	X
Limited Sales Potential						X					X	X	X		X	X	X	X	X	X	X	X	X															
Stable Interactions with Clients												X	X	X	X	X	X	X	X	X	X	X	X															
Friendship Initiation Norms														X	X	X	X	X	X	X	X	X	X															
Emphasis on Sociability												X	X	X	X	X	X	X	X	X	X	X	X							X								
Dancer Self-Regulation												X	X	X	X	X	X	X	X	X	X	X	X															
Emphasis on Performance & Beauty																X	X	X						X	X		X	X	X	X	X	X	X	X	X	X	X	X
Passive Customer Selection Sales														X		X	X	X						X	X	X	X	X	X	X	X	X	X	X	X	X	X	X
Showcasing	X																							X		X	X	X	X	X	X	X	X	X	X	X	X	X
Strict Beauty Standards	X																			X				X	X	X	X	X	X	X	X	X	X	X	X	X	X	X
Strict Enforcement of Policies																								X	X	X	X	X	X	X	X	X	X	X	X	X	X	X
Restricted Customer Dancer Interaction																								X	X	X	X	X	X	X	X	X	X	X	X	X	X	X

focused on making comparisons across the sensitizing concepts of club work and normative orders, sentiment order, and commitment formation. I developed links between categories, attempting to causally link the phenomena to other factors. That is, throughout the course of my data collection and analyses, I made connections between categories in order to specify empirical propositions, asking how these categories related to one another, and investigated these derived explanations in subsequent interviews and observation periods.

What began as a bunch of scribbled notes and a number of tape cassettes soon evolved into a series of piles in my living room. I would arrange them by "concept" or "theme" (asking, "What do these observations have in common? What relationship do these piles have to each other?"). Then, after an interview, observation period, or reading something new, I would completely reorganize them and see if this reorganization led to any new ideas or provided a better explanation of what I was seeing and experiencing.

Any omissions or ambiguities are certainly unintentional and in no way meant to deceive the reader. The longevity of my data collection efforts and the varying sources of information made deciding which exact passages or examples to include extremely difficult. As is typical with qualitative field work, exact enumeration of project participants, observations, and so on seems somewhat artificial. To quantify such concepts as feelings or perceptions as one grasps the general "sense" of an environment is undeniably challenging. Is itemizing the things that I have seen, heard, done, and discerned a contrived effort to boost my research's "scientific" appeal and appear more credible? Ultimately, I opted to provide as much detail as possible, acknowledging that these details are incomplete at best. In their own field research, I encourage my colleagues and kindred academic rogues to further investigate the ideas I put forth here.

THE DANCERS

Much of the information provided in this study is based on formal interview data from fifty female exotic dancers throughout the United States, and informal interviews and field observations involving dozens of others.[2] Dancers ranged in age from eighteen years to approximately forty years old.[3] Approximately 11 percent

of the women interviewed were self-identified as African American. The remaining interview sample self-identified as white, with
the exception of one Asian participant. The average age was 25.5
years. Every effort was made to maximize the variation in respondents and club environment. To this end, dancers were asked questions regarding club(s) where they had been employed as well as
the establishments in which they were currently working.

Participants were also recruited to maximize the variation in
length of career in exotic dance in order to maximize comparisons. Thus, the sample ranges from women who report dancing
one time to those who report having worked in the exotic dance
industry for more than seventeen years. The typical dancer in this
sample reported having been involved in exotic dance for approximately four years.

In addition to variation in length of career, I interviewed
dancers at various stages in their careers. Every attempt was made
to recruit women from each subtype of career stage. That is, I
recruited women who were just beginning their careers as well as
those who were actively involved and maintaining regular employment in the exotic dance industry. Roughly 49 percent of the
women interviewed were currently actively involved in dancing
with no immediate plans to quit; approximately 8 percent of
women reported having danced one time and were unsure about
plans to continue.[4]

I also utilized my associations with club owners and dancers
to recruit former dancers who had effectively "retired"—they
were no longer currently working as dancers nor had any plans to
do so. About 16 percent of respondents were retired dancers.

While soliciting interviews, I also discovered another subtype
of career length, characterized by fluctuation of involvement in
exotic dance careers. These women, whom I label as "oscillators,"
reported periods of steady involvement in exotic dance followed
by periods of noninvolvement. Oscillators, for a variety of reasons, rarely actually retire permanently. Rather, from time to time,
these women quit dancing because of other relationship obligations or to seek other avenues of employment but frequently
return to exotic dancing. Roughly 27 percent of respondents were
classified as oscillators.

Overall, my observations met with little hostility from
dancers. As mentioned, the few reservations they had about my
presence primarily concerned hindering their ability to make

money by having another female there to detract customer attention. In order to allay these concerns, as well as encourage the dancers to speak freely, I often remained in the dressing room to conduct interviews. Not only did this encourage dancers to see me as nonthreatening and to not regard my presence as competition, but this position offered me the unique opportunity to observe more candid dancer interactions and conversations, especially those regarding customers, owners, and other dancers.

Because of my preexisting relationships and prior experiences as a dancer, club owners were frequently either enthusiastic or apathetic about my presence. Only one owner responded to my presence with hostility. After two months of onsite observations and interviews at this establishment, I was removed from the premises due to the owner's perception that I was making the "girls think too much about their lives." I later obtained interviews with almost all dancers from this establishment using alternate methods, such as referral through mutual acquaintances and e-mail referral. I learned that the dancers at this establishment discovered why I had been removed and "got pissed off at him thinking we were sheep." They responded by all agreeing to be interviewed.

What began as my own autobiographical journey developed into something bigger: an inside look at the complexity of sexual labor. Drawing on my own involvement gave me both insight and access to the multiple worlds of exotic dance. But it is not my own story. It is not my goal to simply tell my own adventures. Rather, my aim is to let my own stories, contacts, and insight become tools for capturing dancers' stories and to give depth to descriptions of the varying contexts in which their experiences are embedded.

In the following chapters, I present club typologies based on observations and described by the dancers. Dancers use the term *club* to define a unique type of exotic dance establishment, and subsequently, a unique type of exotic dance experience. Based on their information, I outline the social worlds of each type of club, using an example establishment that is both most frequently defined by this label and shares relevant structural features of all other establishments that were also classified by this reference. In order to preserve the anonymity of all participants and protect all establishments from any and all criminal and civil liabilities, the names and easily identifiable characteristics of all dancers, customers, owners, establishments, and locations have been changed.

I give readers one caveat: this book contains graphic and offensive language. In my experiences with strip clubs, I have come across some of the foulest language I have ever heard. During the selection of interview passages for this book, I contemplated whether or not to modify the vernacular so as to make it more palatable to potential readers. I did tone down the language, but only slightly. Ultimately, I left most of the interviews relatively unaltered, especially those in which dancers describe the experiences of management, fellow dancers, or club environment, as I believe their use of strong language is indicative of the powerful feelings they have regarding their work. To more than modestly modify their words masks the exact variations in emotional intensity this study tries to unravel. They chose these words for a reason; leaving them unchanged gives the reader a better understanding of these dancers and how they think about their work.

3

DANCING AT THE HUSTLE CLUB

It was fall 2000 when I went to work at Spanky's. My two friends and fellow dancers, Coco and Toni, went with me. The club was more than three hours from where we lived, but we hoped that a club in a bigger city would guarantee us enough profit to make the drive worth it. During the previous week, Coco had called the club to ask if they were hiring dancers and to see if the manager would agree to let the three of us work if we drove out there. The manager she spoke with must have been able to tell by her voice that she was African American. He asked her if all of us were black. She told him that she was black, but Toni and I were white. "Good," he said, "'Cuz we don't hire a lot of black girls." He told her that the owner did not think black women were a good commodity and that he was not sure if she would be allowed to work or not. She would have to be "a really hot black girl" to get hired.

The three of us showed up on a Friday, around 6:00 p.m. We walked in and asked to speak with the manager and audition. Frankie, a huge, portly, bald man in a dark suit with an unbuttoned shirt walked over and introduced himself. He then told us we would have to go on stage and dance immediately, although no one was there, to "see our bodies . . . to see if we were hot enough." We went on stage all at once and danced for one song. As we came off, Frankie told us that we had passed the test. He told Coco she was hot "for a brown girl." He said I had "great tits" and told Toni she was fine. He told us to put our things in the dressing room.

29

The dressing room was packed, full of dancers getting ready for the upcoming shift. As the three of us walked in, the room went silent. We were met with eye rolling and sneers from other women. In the background, I heard comments like, "Great, some more fucking bitches," and, "Just what we need, more damn dancers." The dressing room was cramped and smoky, with nowhere to really stand or sit and no place to put our things. Toni looked at me with open-mouthed terror. *These women are awful*, her eyes said. I tried to initiate conversation, hoping to ease the tension and optimistically show them we were friendly. This was their turf, I thought, so we should play nice. "Hi, ladies," I said cheerfully. "We're new. This is our first night."

A dancer (later identified as Brianna) rolled her eyes again. "Look, bitches, this dressing room is too small for your shit. This is my space. Don't touch my shit and stay out of my way. This room is for the old school girls only. So why don't you get your asses up to the other dressing room?"

We grabbed our bags and ran upstairs to the other dressing room. We were met with the same greeting. As we huddled in the tiniest open spot, I looked around at the other dancers getting ready. All of their bags had huge locks. Some were even chained to the pipes and tables. I squeezed my way to the bathroom at the end of the hall. In the corner, in front of the toilets, a dancer stood leaning over a makeshift dressing table. She swallowed a pill with beer, looked up at me, and glared. "This is my fucking spot. I've been dancing here for five years, and this is my goddamned space, whether or not I'm here."

"Look, I just want to use the bathroom."

"Whatever." She huffed as she exited, "Bitch."

After I dressed, I went downstairs to discuss the rules. I learned the club was keeping all the money for my first three dances, and I had to pay a "stage fee" of $50 to work that first night. I was also required to tip each bouncer, doorman, and deejay $10. So I started my evening at least $150 in the hole.

"What are the rules about what customers can and can't do?" I asked. Frankie said, "Y'know. No prostitution and all that. Girls vary about how comfortable they are with guys touching. When giving dances in the lap-dance room, try to keep guys' hands off your tits or ass. In the champagne room, some girls are fine with having their asses or tits touched; just don't let guys put their finger in you." I also learned that, in champagne rooms, sometimes "good tippers" were allowed to take off their shirts. These customers tipped heavily to have dancers rub their breasts and genitals over their bare chests.

Most of the girls stood around the deejay booth all night, waiting and trying to get on stage. The stage was an assembly line, filled with dancers. As each new dancer came out, she moved to the end of the stage, and the other dancers scooted down. She stripped completely naked immediately and began squatting on the stage in front of the customers. Dancers had to move quickly, as the assembly line kept adding women to the end of the stage. Women were lined up, elbow to elbow. With no room to dance, the routine went as follows: dancers stood in front of a guy, squatted, and spread their legs wide open. The customer would lean over and look at the dancers' genital areas for a while; many women touched their vaginas for the customer. Dancers then pulled their garters away from their thighs, so customers could place dollars in them. Dancers then stood up and went to the next customer. This process was repeated fifty to sixty times until dancer reached the end of the stage.

I tried for two hours to get on stage, but the deejay kept telling me he had too many other girls in ahead of me. I turned up my southern accent and flirted with a bouncer who had a soft spot for southern redheads. He spoke with the deejay and got me on stage. As I prepared to go on, the bouncer warned me, "You gotta keep moving. Just get the dollar and go. If you have time, go for another buck or two. But the other dancers will try and make you move too fast, 'cuz they want all the money. So defend your spot, but keep up the pace." I walked to the end of the stage, and, like the dozens of women before me, stripped completely naked. The stage was swamped with men, all hooting and hollering. I stood there, not knowing exactly what to do. The customer in front of me shouted, "get down here and show me your pussy." I looked over at a fellow dancer at the end of a smaller stage to my right. She was lying flat on her back, completely naked, with her ankles behind her head. She was holding open her labia, while a group of men towered over her. I winced and turned away. My night had begun.

After I exited the stage, I went to "hustle dances." This meant trying to talk men into going upstairs to buy lap-dances. The typical method is to convince them you'd love to "ride them"—lie on top of them and grind your pelvis on their penis through their jeans. After several attempts, I finally got my first customer. I took him up to the lap-dance room, a room filled with recliner-like chairs. The room was covered with men, each laying flat on their backs, with naked women writhing and grinding on top of them. My customer paid the room attendant twenty dollars, and laid back on an empty recliner. He was young and well dressed, so I was hopeful that he was going to be respectful—those hopes were short lived. As I lay across him and began moving my hips, he began talking dirty. "You like that, don't you? I could . . . Show me . . . Grind that . . . on me." For the next four minutes, he said the most disgusting things I had ever heard—a torrential rain of vulgarity. As I listened to all the ways he would like to sodomize me, I focused on keeping his hands in place and pretending I was having fun. I laughed off his comments by responding with, "Oh hush." "You're so bad." "You have a dirty mouth, don't you, sweetie?"

Afterward, I wanted to run, but I needed to sell another dance. I knew I had a paying customer and did not want to waste time going back downstairs to try to hustle another guy. It had taken what seemed like forever to get this one, and I hated the idea of walking around hustling for an hour to get another. I had repeatedly been grabbed and fondled as I walked among the crowd of packed-in customers. Plus, I needed to sell another two dances just to break even and start making any money. So I acted sorry that our time was up, trying to be dumb and pouty. I made a cute, childlike face and said it was a shame that we were done. I asked if he wanted to "go again." He did.

By the end of the night, my left leg was swollen from a pulled hamstring; the muscle had been pulled so badly that my left thigh was turning purple and was visibly larger than my right. A bouncer helped me hobble out and had to practically carry me down the stairs. My knees were beaten and bruised from getting up and down from a squatting position on stage. They hurt badly from overextending them, and my feet were covered with blisters. My fingernails and toenails were black with filth from walking around a grimy club floor in open-toed shoes and rolling around on a stage that was covered with the sweat, dirt, and body fluids of dozens of other women. My back was killing me from overarching and simulating sex, and my thighs ached from straddling horny men. I had friction burns on my inner thighs from "dry humping" men's jeans for hours. I reeked of cigarette smoke and sweat. I had been licked, touched, propositioned. I had been kicked in the head by a fellow dancer on stage for "not moving fast enough." One of my costumes had been stolen.

I went to collect my money for the private dance from the lap-dance attendant. I had been keeping count on a piece of paper wrapped in my garter and knew I had sold thirty dances and three champagne rooms. The room attendant said I had only sold twenty-seven dances and refused to pay me for all of them (no doubt pocketing the extra cash). We argued, and he called the manager over. The manager said, "Look, he got twenty-seven dances written, not thirty. So take money for the twenty-seven, or take none. That's it. I don't want to hear it." I took the money for the twenty-seven dances. I was then smugly reminded that I was also required to tip all lap-dance attendants ten dollars. I handed over the ten dollars.

As we loaded the car, I looked at Toni and Coco. They had had the same type of evening I had just experienced. We all looked at each other the way people do when they have been through a natural disaster: we were dazed, bruised piles of smeared makeup, ratty hair, and body odor. But our garters were filled with cash. Even after paying our stage fees and required house fees and tipping three bouncers, a deejay, and two lap-dance room attendants, we had each made a lot of money.

On the way home, none of us spoke. We drove the three hours home in complete silence—no talking, no radio. Each of us was an otherwise self-identified chatterer, yet we were speechless. As I dropped them off, we barely mumbled goodbye. When I got home, I immediately hobbled into a scalding hot shower, scrubbing my body repeatedly. I fell into bed feeling ashamed and dirty. I had made a lot of money. In fact, all three of us had been dancers for years, and each of us had made the most money ever for a single night's work. And it was perhaps the worst night of my life.

But this was not my typical experience dancing. In fact, it was contrary to my entire definition of what dancing meant. My past experiences at other establishments had defined the roles and expectations of being a dancer. And working at this club was a stark contrast with that definition. Although there are certainly a number of these clubs, I had never worked in one before. Rather, I had worked in other types of clubs, and there was a vast difference here in what I had come to expect and what I understood dancing to mean. What it meant to be a dancer in this establishment was to be frustrated and powerless, devalued and exploited.

I was trash; I was worthless; I was an object to be used, both by the men and by the management.

Clearly this experience was degrading for me and for the rest of the women working there. What made working there so awful? The horrible experience seemed to be based on how dancing was defined. The way this club was organized created this culture. The structure, management, language, formal policies, and informal rules create a social world in which dancers were devalued, sexually harassed, and exploited. And they adapted to these conditions by giving up and directing their frustrations at themselves and their fellow dancers.

In the following paragraphs I present the social organization that constitutes a "hustle club." That is, I outline the properties of social world context of being an exotic dancer in this type of establishment. I focus on physical description of the club, temporality of interactions, relative power, method of money making, and overall image promoted by the management. I then discuss the relationship between these structural characteristics and career persistence. Specifically, I explain how the organizational features of each club affect dancers' perceptions of work and attitudes toward fellow dancers, customers, management, and subsequent experiences of work.

THE SOCIAL WORLD OF THE HUSTLE CLUB

The following description outlines the structural features, individual perceptions and adjustments, and career continuity patterns of a typical hustle club. My description uses a fictitious name, *The Pussycat* to refer to clubs of this sort. This one club name represents a number of clubs, similar in organizational features. That is, rather than being one club, *The Pussycat* represents a *type* of club, a type of social world, a type of dancing experience.[1]

The Pussycat

The Pussycat is a large club located in the "red light" district of a large industrial city. The club has been sold several times and has gone through number of different managers. Having little contact with management, many of the dancers are not sure of the rank of authority and are unclear about whether any of the managers may be the club owner. "I think Phil owns the place, but Jason's supposed to be runnin' it. They're always here in the upstairs office, countin' the cash and not being bothered. So, I'm not sure. The only time I see any of them is when they're yelling at us or giving us [the dancers] shit. So I just stay outta the way and make my money" (Tia, twenty-four, danced two years).

It is a large club in terms of both physical layout and dancer population. The downstairs section of the building consists of a dressing room, one large main stage, and two smaller stages (referred to as "second and "third stage"). The number of women working on any given night varies greatly, ranging from between fifty to sixty on a weeknight to more than seventy on a weekend. There are usually between twenty and thirty women on the main stage and between five and ten women on each of the lower stages at any given time. Upstairs is the lap-dance room, holding approximately twenty laid-back recliners, and several champagne rooms.

The dancer turnover rate is very high. There is no scheduling, and the composition of the dancer population varies greatly on any given night. Every dancer must pay a fee upon arrival in order to work; this "stage fee" is typically twenty-five to fifty dollars. Women are free to come and go as they please, beginning or ending their work schedule whenever they so choose, as long as the stage fee is paid.

The Pussycat has a large and diverse clientele, including a variety of ages, races, and economic statuses, with few "regular" customers. Customers are almost exclusively male, there alone as well as in groups or pairs. Club management estimates that there are approximately three hundred men there on any given weeknight; this estimate approximately doubles on weekends. Each customer must pay a twenty-five dollar cover charge, pass through a metal detector, and undergo a quick "pat-down" search prior to entering the club area.

For both the club and the dancers, the primary method of making money is through the selling of lap dances and champagne rooms. Lap dances typically cost between twenty and forty dollars; of this, the club makes roughly 50 percent. Champagne rooms range in price from about one hundred fifty dollars for fifteen minutes to two hundred dollars for a half-hour; of this, the dancer usually makes only forty and seventy-five dollars, respectively. The Pussycat's management requires dancers to sell as many dances as possible, usually taking all profits for the first two lap dances sold per dancer each night. The first night a dancer works, the club keeps the profits from three dances.

The club atmosphere emphasizes sexual gratification. Throughout the night, deejays, lap-dance attendants, and management make references to female sexual organs when talking about dancers. Slang terms for female sexual organs are frequently spoken over the microphone. For example, as a dancer steps on to the stage, the deejay will announce, "Hey guys, take a look at the tits on this gal." Similarly, dancers are often referred to with phrases such as "hot piece of ass."

Because of the large number of dancers, there is no systematic order of placement on stage. Rather, through the instruction of the management, dancers who make the club the most money have the highest priority for getting stage time. This is used as an incentive to motivate women to boost sales in order to have the opportunity to make an appearance on stage. Appearing on stage offers both the immediate benefit of receiving on-stage tips as well as drawing the attention of potential customers who may then be pursued to purchase lap dances and champagne rooms.

However, the nature of stage placement creates a cyclical pattern of unfair advantage among some dancers. Those who appear on stage receive more exposure and are therefore more likely to sell dances and champagne rooms; these sales ensure that they will continue to be selected for stage time in the future. Subsequently, those who are new to the club or, for some reason or another, are not initially selling a lot of dances, face the added difficulty of competing to sell future dances without having been on stage.

In addition, because the dancers are called to the stage by the deejay, the deejay has some freedom as to which dancers he or she can call. As a consequence, stage time is often determined by which dancer has given the deejay the biggest tip.

There are large numbers of dancers nightly; thus, customers feel justified in "shopping around" to select which dancer they find most appealing. Inevitably, they begin asking to see the dancers fully nude before making their selection. This practice, referred to as "checking out the merchandise," often makes selling even more difficult for women who have not been previously selected for placement on stage. Many dancers report being more aggressive with customers and deejays in order to overcome this disadvantage and deal with the frustration of not being able to make money by getting on stage.

When not on stage, dancers must walk around among the crowds of customers to hustle dances. Often, a customer will ask dancers to "flash him," with the promise that if he likes the "merchandise," he will buy a dance. Sometimes the customer does intend to buy a dance, yet sometimes he does not, and enjoys the free show. Dancers know this is often the case yet feel compelled to comply with any requests to display themselves naked to solicit dances. The women feel they must do whatever they have to so as to sell as many dances as possible in order to recoup their initial club costs and make money. One dancer summarizes her experience:

> I gave up trying to get on stage. But the guys wanna see you naked before they'll buy a dance, so I just flash them right there on the floor (the area around the stage where customers congregate). I show 'em that I don't have a shitty body or some third tit or somethin' and then try to talk 'em into a dance. I used to try to get on stage, but it was a pain in the ass, and I spent all my time standing there waiting while he sent some other bitch up instead of me—when I've been there waiting for a damned hour! Other girls get pissed off about it, 'cuz you're not supposed to be naked when you're working the floor. But it's harder for a guy to say "no" when a naked woman's standing there grinding on you, and he's got his hands on your ass. The women on stage bitch that I'm stealing their customers. [But] I gotta make money. I don't have time for that. (Trixie, twenty-six, danced three years)

Whereas one interaction strategy entails being more sexually open to potential customers, another available negotiation involves being more aggressive toward the deejay:

> It's damn near impossible to get on stage. You've either gotta be blowin' Frankie (the owner) or deejay or giving the damn deejay all your money. Either that, or you've gotta be a real bitch. If you're a big enough bitch, the deejay will be scared or pissed off and give you your way just to get rid of you. (Tia, twenty-four, danced two years)

You gotta be a bitch to get on stage. I was waiting up
there one time forever. Then I just snapped. I went off on
the deejay, screaming and shit and calling him a fucking
asshole . . . The manager came over 'cuz we were really
getting into it . . . [The manager] told the deejay to just
put me on the damn stage so I'd shut up. Now I just cut
out the middle-man. I'm a bitch from the get go, so I
don't have to waste my time. I gave up being nice to that
ass. And now I am on stage at least three or four times a
night. (Toy, twenty-four, danced six years)

The difficulty of getting on stage and the club's emphasis on
lap-dance and champagne-room sales as the primary method of
money making mean that most of the women spend very little
time on stage. They spend most of their time among the crowd of
customers, soliciting dances.

The formal club policy states that there is no touching
allowed while a dancer is on stage. However, many dancers
report that being grabbed or fondled is typical while moving
unsupervised among the crowd of customers trying to sell dances.
The lack of concern for individual dancer well-being is exempli-
fied by management's nonenforcement of touching policies.
Touching of the dancers is not policed, and violations of the
posted "no touching" policy are underenforced or capriciously
enforced. Furthermore, the continual sexual reference to women's
genitalia by club staff encourages customers to transgress physical sexual boundaries. Constant references to "those hot tits" or
"that tight ass" portray women as objects for sexual gratification
rather than as dancers.

The combination of repeated sexual referencing and the disregard for individual dancers acts so that women are continually
working in an environment that tolerates, if not encourages,
sexual harassment. One dancer stated, "Every guy you pass cops a
feel. They all feel no reservation about grabbing your ass or your
tits when you walk by. Shit, I've come to expect it." Similarly,
there is no policy regarding touching during lap dances or while in
the champagne room.

Hustle clubs are establishments, according to dancers, that use
dancers and primarily use conning, or "hustling," to making
money. When I asked women in these types of clubs to define their

jobs, they repeatedly stated that their job was using manipulation and swindling to encourage customers to spend money or to spend more than they had actually intended. Dancers used phrases such as "conning men," "smooth talking," or "working them [customers] over" to describe their jobs. The club promotes using these techniques; women are encouraged by management to lie to customers, mislead them, or suggest to them that they will become sexually satisfied if they continue to spend money.

In an interview with Bonni, a long-time dancer at a hustle club, she characterized her job responsibilities:

> Well, I try to take every dollar a man's got. I sweet talk him and convince him that if he'll just spend a little more, he's going to get off [ejaculate]. The hard part is making the first sell. Men don't always want to make the leap to a lap dance: they start off cheap. But usually once I get a guy to agree to a dance, I'm in. It's easier to get him to buy another than it is to get that first one. But once the credit card is out, it's out, and what's another twenty dollars? And another twenty dollars? I just keep making it more intense—grinding harder and letting him get away with more—so he's always thinking that one more dance will do the trick. And he's spent a couple hundred bucks before you know it.

I asked Bonni if she felt any guilt about using these techniques.

> Hell no. They deserve it for me putting up with their shit. He's using me, so I'm using him. And I gotta make money. This guy doesn't give a shit about me, so why should I worry about his feelings? [Sarcastically] Poor baby, thought you were gonna fuck me like some whore, and I lied to you. How bad of me. Whatever. I gotta make money; I don't have time to care. I don't want to waste time trying to go get another one [customer] either. The clock is ticking. It sucks going around damn near begging guys to please let me ride you and getting shut down. They look you up and down, deciding if you're worth their lousy twenty dollars. Like I'm a piece of meat at the grocery store. And I'm just hoping they decide my body

and face are good enough to grind on their lap. So screw
them. I got one here, and I'm finally making money, so
I'm keeping him as long as I can however I need to.

ADJUSTING TO THE WORLD OF THE HUSTLE CLUB

The structural features of the hustle club, including the large numbers of dancers and customers, the emphasis on sex, and unin-
volved management, create a hostile, competitive, and isolating
environment. Because there is a constant inflow and outflow of
dancers and customers, any one individual woman is expendable.
Subsequently, the management feels no need to negotiate with her,
improve her working conditions, or protect her safety. The management strategy lets dancers know that there will always be
another dancer willing to work and that the club will run just as
smoothly with fifty-nine dancers as it will with sixty. This management philosophy emanates through to the deejays and bouncers.
The underenforcement of no-touching policies and the low com-
mission that results from club profit-division practices create the
context in which women feel frustrated, powerless, and exploited.
     The large, constant turnover and lack of concern or involve-
ment with management, deejays, and bouncers signal dancers that
they are replaceable; dancers in this social world know that they
are regarded as nuisances, and their concerns will be easily dis-
missed. The stress of meeting quotas and selling dances as the primary method of making money creates a very competitive
atmosphere among the dancers. This focus on competition, in con-
junction with a disinterested, hands-off management style, characterized by lack of policy creation or enforcement regarding
touching, promotes hostility among dancers. Dancers are essentially left to themselves to fight over resources. In this world, they
feel that they are on their own, defending their bodies and scram-
bling for money.
     This hostility is exacerbated by management tolerance of ram-
pant drug use among dancers. Dancers frequently reported that
management did nothing to control or prohibit drug use among
dancers; open use of cocaine, marijuana, and ecstasy was frequently reported, and dancers often stated that drug/alcohol use
was essential in order to deal with the stress of working in this
environment.

Jamison, a dancer for roughly eight months, stated:

When I first started, I was nervous about rolling [using ecstasy] or anything while I was working. But I really needed a pill or something to get through the night. I have to take the edge off. It's just so stressful.

M: What's so stressful about working here? Can you tell me more about your stress?

Everything. The men suck. The management is scary. They just yell at you if you're not making money and fire girls at will. Total assholes. And the women here are awful. I've got a friend, and we started together, so we agreed to watch each other's back. But these girls are trash. They're total cunts.

The drug use frequently reported in hustle clubs not only made fellow dancers more hostile but increased their willingness to steal. In addition, dancers stated that inebriated dancers often were unable or unwilling to maintain physical boundaries with customers. As a consequence, dancers indicated that it was more difficult for them to maintain physical boundaries with customers when competing with other dancers who were "messed up" (intoxicated or "high"). The following quote demonstrates the hostility and frustration that can result from management's disregard for both drug use and touching:

I go upstairs to do a lap [perform a lap dance] with this guy, and there's Barbi, all fucked up. And the guy she's with is all fuckin' over her . . . [S]he's whacked outta her mind and he's sucking all over her and squeezing her tits and shit. You can just tell she's fuckin' outta her mind . . . rollin' her damn face off [taking ecstasy] . . . Now the guy I got thinks he's gonna pull that shit with me, and of course, when I'm not down like that, he's gonna get pissed and leave after one dance. And you know Franco [the club manager/owner] doesn't give a fuck. He lets her sleep it off in one of the [champagne] rooms all the time . . . I'm fine with whatever she wants to do. If she wants to fucking rot her brain, I don't care. These bitches can all get messed up if they want. But now she's fucking with my money. (Chelsea, twenty-seven, danced six years)

In addition, management has greater relative power and is subsequently less willing to negotiate with her. When there is an ever-ready supply of dancers, the management does not recognize any individual identity: dancers become nameless and faceless. It is then easier to fire any individual dancer than to negotiate. Dancers indicated that they were aware of their relative lack of power and lack of individual identity in negotiations with management.

> We're a dime a dozen here. Jason [the manager] says that all the time. Like, if one girl [is] giving him shit, he'll put up with it, but only for a little while, and only if she's making the club a lot of money. Then he'll just fuckin' fire her. (Toni, twenty-four, danced six years)

> I saw him [Jason] one night, screaming at Venus. She'd worked here for a while, and they got into it over her dances. She says she sold more than he was paying her for. I seriously think she was getting ripped off, and Jason was not paying her for all her sales. She started with him, and he just screamed at her, calling her a fucking bitch and telling her to get the fuck out, that he had tons of girls, and she didn't mean shit . . . She left crying and asking him to please let her work. We were all on pins and needles that night, just trying to stay outta the way . . . She eventually begged him enough that he let her come back. (Korene, twenty-four, danced four years)

The organization of the hustle club creates a social world in which exotic dancing is defined as the buying and selling of women for male sexual gratification. This image of what exotic dancing is means that any individual dancer is merely a product to be bought and sold. The social organization of the hustle club creates an environment in which the objectification and degradation of women is permissible, if not encouraged. In this social world, it is permissible for women to be disrespected, violated, and abused.

Dancer descriptions of hustle clubs illustrate the depersonalized environment:

> I hate it so much. We're just T and A ["tits and ass"]. It's like a meat market. (Toni, twenty-four, danced six years)

It's like a big assembly line. Each of us comes out, goes to the end, and the others move down. We spend the whole time squatting with our legs spread open. Eventually I think the guys get bored too. There's only so much pussy you can look at 'til they all look the same, and a guy'll just pick one [for a lap dance] at random. (Tia, twenty-four, danced two years)

I only worked there a couple of times. I spent the whole night laying in front of the guys and spreading my legs wide open. Guys never even look you in the face; they just stare at one pussy after another. I made a shitload of cash, but I cried all the way home. The money was sooo good, but I just couldn't go back. Just thinking about it makes me sick. (Sierra, twenty-seven, danced five years)

These quotes illustrate that, among dancers in hustles clubs, being a dancer is being powerless; a dancer's sexuality is an object to be bought and sold. Nearly all of the dancers at hustle clubs reported that they were regarded as "T and A," rather than as individual people. As one dancer, Toni, summarizes:

I know you wanna know whether stripping is bad for women. Yeah, it is. At least it is here. After I leave this place, I go home and scrub my entire body in burning hot water, then I have my boyfriend hold me and make love. Not fuck—I can't be fucked after goin' there 'cuz I feel like that's what I've been doin' all night. I need to be affirmed.
M: What do you mean by "affirmed"?
He makes love to me and talks sweet. I need to feel like a person—like being a woman is good again. Maybe I'm just a little crazy or somethin'. I need to be affirmed that I'm someone who is loved and worth somethin'.

The above paragraph illustrates how the social organization of the hustle club has a powerful effect of the meaning of dancing. The high turnover rate of customers and dancers, and corresponding absence of meaningful personal interactions, creates an environment characterized by hostility and conflict and lack of personal identity. Being a dancer in this environment means being objectified and degraded; thus, being successful in this environment requires dancers to accept this devalued status.

Dancers consistently stated that "getting tough" was a necessary and unavoidable negotiation strategy in order to adjust to this environment. That is, in order to continue to work in an atmosphere in which they feel frustrated, objectified, and powerless, women develop an aggressive or hostile demeanor. However, due to their relative lack of power with management (they can easily be fired) and inability to act out against customers (they must be polite in order to persuade customers to buy dances), dancers most frequently vent their frustrations with both the competition and the only available outlet: their fellow dancers. Thus, there is a general atmosphere of open antagonism among dancers. "All the women are bitches. Fuck 'em! I pay my bills and handle my business. They can fuck off" (Francesca, twenty-one, danced one year).

The lack of management involvement creates an atmosphere of normlessness. Essentially, there are no rules. Drug use, sexual harassment, and solicitation are commonplace; theft is an everyday occurrence that goes unpunished. All the women in hustle clubs reported that they had personal items, clothing, or money stolen from them or had witnessed theft occurring against another dancer. All dancers reported using locks to secure their items in dressing rooms. One dancer stated that in addition to using locks, she secured her belongings in a padlocked trunk chained to a post in the dressing room. The following excerpt demonstrates the dancers' sense of lawlessness and subsequent aggressive and proactive adjustment:

> You gotta watch your back around here. I only work when Holly comes with me. A girl in here by herself— man, the other girls will make her life hell. You gotta have backup, someone making sure you're not having your clothes and bags fucked with or your shit stolen. My first night, I came here with three other girls, and three of us had shit stolen. Now we all watch each other's shit all the time—lock everything, and keep your money on you at all times. Bitches will cut open your dance bag if they think you may have money in there. (Mandi, danced two years)

Moreover, it seems that this adaptation to degradation and powerlessness becomes more pervasive the longer a dancer stays in this social world, such that the longer a dancer has worked in the hustle club, the "harder" she becomes. In some instances, long-time dancers have been intensely hostile to their competitors, engaging in behavior that could be considered cruel:

> I remember the one time this new girl came in. There are always tons of new girls, but for some reason Brianna decided to pick on her. She [Brianna] was fuckin' vicious, man. She and a number of the other old school girls were awful. They ripped into her dance bag and took all her shit. One of those skanks even pissed in this chick's dance bag, Brianna put her cigarette out in the girl's makeup bag. They were calling her names and shit, threatening to kick her ass. Brianna knew they could get away with it, 'cuz Jason didn't fuckin' give a shit. Brianna sells a lot of dances, so Jason won't do shit. I knew it then, man: stay away from the bitch [Brianna] . . . she's a fuckin' snake. (Korene, twenty-four, danced four years)

In my interview with Jamison, she described her fellow dancers as "awful." I asked her to describe what they do that makes them so terrible.

> They steal your shit, lie to customers about you. I've heard girls telling customers, "Oh, stay away from her. She has AIDs. Get a dance with me instead." Or they'll tell a guy that a girl's boyfriend or husband is here, when he's not, just so the customer will be scared off and buy a dance with them instead of her . . . That's some shady shit, to tell lies and shit, but they all do it. Cut each other's throats for twenty dollars.

Brianna's Story

Brianna was a twenty-seven-year-old dancer. She had been dancing about nine years, usually a few nights a week. She dropped out of high school during her senior year and began dancing after

working a series of low-paying jobs. Brianna had had a number
of long-term, live-in boyfriends. She was the mother of three children. One child was fathered by a previous boyfriend; she blamed
their breakup on their mutual drug and alcohol use. Her current
boyfriend and father of her two younger children was unem-
ployed, having recently quit his job at a local factory. Brianna
described her childhood as

> pretty normal . . . [M]y folks were fine. I wasn't abused or
> anything—pretty normal. My parents were divorced, and
> I lived with my mom, but I saw my dad all the time.
>
> Well, where do I begin? I been dancing since I was
> eighteen. I'm from Steelton. I started dancing right after
> high school. It was easy money. I was eighteen and didn't
> know shit. I sure as hell wasn't getting no nine to five or
> nothin' like that. I waitressed for a while and worked at
> Burger King. Then my boyfriend was always going to the
> strip club with his friends, so I figured what the hell? . . . I
> got up there and started making some cash. That's it. I
> quit the other shitty jobs right after that. Here I could get
> fucked up and party all night and still get paid. Shit, why
> not?

Brianna described dancing at the Pussycat:

> It's hard work. It was easier at first, because I was so
> fucked up that shit didn't matter. I'd just get shit faced
> every night. No kids, just partying. I was eighteen, nine-
> teen years old. And I didn't give a shit about anything. I
> didn't feel bad about the shit that goes on around here,
> because I was so focused on making money and getting
> high.
>
> M: What do you mean by "the shit that goes on?"
> Could you tell me more about that?
>
> Well, you know. The tricking [prostitution] and all,
> the guys being assholes, getting screwed over by manage-
> ment. I didn't even think about that shit. I mean, even
> after the house [club] got all that money off me, I'd still
> make more than I ever had. And no one cared that I was
> fucked up.

M: How do you feel about your job now?

I think it was the worst thing I ever did. It was so easy at first—quick money and drugs. But now I'm screwed. I've got kids now and can't get fucked up, so now it's a lot harder to put up with all the shit here, men trying to get on you and shit, guys jerking off or trying to fuck you. The women are total bitches. They'll steal your customer, your clothes, your money. And I fucking hate Frankie and Jay. They stiff me for dances and champagnes after I bust my ass all night.

M: Have you ever thought about quitting?

I've quit a hundred times. I just get sick of this place. I'm burned out. I been doing this shit too long. I'm sick of all these assholes. I loved the club I started in, but I moved back to Pilottown to be with my kids' daddy. I fucking hate it here. The management is totally ripping us off. But I can't afford to not be workin.' My old man ain't worth shit. Like, last week, he was supposed to pick up something for my son's fucking birthday. But his sorry ass sure as hell didn't have the money. So who do you think was here bustin' her ass to throw the kid a party? Me. Then he's always givin' me shit about workin' here. Nigga's ass has no problem spending my money, does he? I told him if he would get a real fuckin' job then I would-n't have to do this crap. When he starts paying my bills, he can have a damned opinion . . .

And the guys are assholes . . . always trying to fuck-ing touch you and shit, tryin' for blow jobs. And the whores around here are doing it. The women here are all bitches. That's the worst part. I'm working some guy all night, and some bitch steals him, probably offering to suck his dick or something. I'll kick some bitch's ass if she steals my trick. Just watch her try and get up in my face. I'll go off.

M: What would you do if you weren't dancing?

Sitting my ass at home would be what I'd wanna do, but probably factory or some shit like that. Flipping burg-ers? I quit all the time. We tell my kids that I'm a waitress. That's probably what I'd do. I worked at a bar before, last time I quit.

Brianna's customers saw her only as an object for their sexual gratification; consequently they felt justified sexually harassing her. She had to continually struggle to maintain her physical boundaries and deal with sexual coercion. Not only did management not respond to her needs, but management practices exacerbated her situation. She was not cared about; she was simply an anonymous dancer, just like all the others. She could not complain; she had to tolerate their unfair working conditions and management policies. Her coworkers also intensified her feeling of hostility and frustration; they were threats to the livelihood that she struggled to earn.

In response to these circumstances, Brianna became aggressive to her fellow dancers. She lacked the power to confront her employer (she might lose her job) and her customers (they were essential for money making). However, because all dancers share essentially equivalent relative power, she could channel her frustrations and resentment into her interactions with fellow colleagues. Brianna's story illustrates how the club environment defines the nature of her work. Being a hustler means being devalued and frustrated. Specific dancer adjustment strategies, and subsequent perceptions of work, are influenced by the social organization of the hustle club. Her work atmosphere was competitive and sexually emphasized, characterized by management apathy and dancer disposability.

Brianna's story is highly representative of the conditions, perceptions, and situational adjustments of hustle club dancers. Dancers at hustle clubs most often described their occupation using negative terminology.

Did I go back to a hustle club? Yes, I did. I had had the worst experience of my life, and I went back to the Pussycat and to many other clubs just like it. Am I crazy for subjecting myself to that again? Maybe. Perhaps I was a bit too ambitious as a novice ethnographer, but I felt I had to go back to confirm that what I experienced was real and validate that my night there was neither unique for me nor ungeneralizable to the other women there. I had to be sure that that club was not an anomaly and wanted to interview the dancers working there. I had secretly hoped that the Pussycat would be a one-of-a-kind establishment and that dancing was truly not "really" like this for anyone beyond this limited number of women. But, as you can see, my Pussycat experience was not the only one of its kind.

4

DANCING AT THE SHOW CLUB

I was extremely nervous as I walked into Divas. When I had called the previous week to inquire about dancing, I was asked my height, weight, measurements, date of birth, bra cup size, and hair color. I was told the club owner would see if they had any openings. He called and scheduled my audition for that evening. I was told to bring a g-string, platform heels, and a garter. I was referred to the local lingerie store in town. I was advised that, prior to auditioning I needed to "buy a real dancer's costume, made for professional dancers. No cheap shit or house clothes."

Upon entering the club, I was greeted by the manager, Huey. Huey gave me an employment application and a contract. The contract stipulated that I would not dance at any another club while I was employed there. It also stated that I could be fired at any time without reason. Huey read an extensive list of club policies involving scheduling. He then told me to stop back into the office after my audition so he could take a picture of me in my costume to add to my file and application. He informed me that "they have some strict rules here" and that "they don't just hire anyone . . . Divas has the best-looking women in the area . . . so you shouldn't take it personal if you don't get hired. But let's wait and see how the audition goes."

The dressing room was large, with a series of tables and lighted mirrors. Each seat had a counter, with various beauty products provided by the club. There were a number of lockers, many with full-length mirrors on the doors. I took off my jacket, hung it on the coat rack, and took an open seat at a dressing table.

Several women looked up and nodded, then immediately went back to diligently fixing their hair and makeup, painting their nails, or organizing their costumes for the evening.

"Hello. I'm new and have no idea what I'm doing. Can you let me know how it works here?" I asked the dancer next to me (later identified as Vegas), with a tone of desperation. Vegas began giving me the "way it works" speech, as she continued gluing on fake eyelashes and sticking small costume jewels to her face and body. No touching at all, no talking to the customers while not on stage. When not on stage or giving a lap dance, all dancers are supposed to be in the dressing room. No walking around the club, soliciting dances. All music selections must be turned in to the deejay at least one set before you are due to be on stage.

I was advised of the absolute essentials of dancing: baby wipes, fake tanning lotion, body spray cologne, and stage makeup. "You should wipe your body with the wipes as much as possible. And I spray perfume before every set. You have to be squeaky clean if you're going to be naked up there. You want to smell sweet and flowery as much as possible . . . Fake tanner and Dermablend will hide any cellulite, stretch marks . . . moles, tattoos."

Although most of the other women ignored me, Starri, a relatively new dancer piped in, "Oh, and you should probably spend everything you make the first week or so on costumes and shoes. Beautiful costumes are essential. They're expensive, but you want to look good. You want to look like a real dancer. It's part of the performance. It's just an investment you gotta make."

As I changed into my "professional costume," which I had just purchased for ninety dollars the night before, I listened to the conversations around me, which centered primarily on weight loss, diet pills, and beauty products. "Can you tell I've lost weight? I've been really hitting the gym. I was a size five, and now I'm like a three. Can you tell? I want to lose more, but I don't want my boobs to get too small." Dancers exchanged advice on the best way to drop weight and reduce bloating and covered such topics as a "special tea that helps you lose weight. If you take it with a couple Ex-Lax, you'll just shit out everything you eat. It just goes right through . . . I've been doing it every day for a week, and I've lost, like, five pounds!" Another dancer sang the praises of a new tanning lotion "that gets super hot, so you get really dark, especially in those ultrafast beds."

The most important advice I learned from Starri? "Never, ever copy someone—their music, costumes, or moves. Don't do what they do on the pole or try and dance like they do or play their songs. Girls will get mad at you. You won't fit in here if you do that."

I turned my music in to the deejay, sat at the top of the stairs overlooking the stage, and waited for my turn. I watched the dancer on stage before me and knew there was absolutely no way I could copy her. She was tall, platinum blonde, extremely tanned, and had enormous fake breasts. Her costume was bright red and covered with sequins. Her hair, skin, face, and body were flawless. Her demeanor exuded confidence and commanded attention. Her eyes and her stride radiated power. She was arrogant, yet completely enthralling. Her body, face, mannerisms, movement, and attitude were all mesmerizing. I was struck by the perfection of the entire performance. It was perfect in a way that does not occur in nature, artificially perfect. Normal people just do not look or act like that.

As the smoke machine filled the stage and the strobe light flickered, she climbed to the top of the sixty-foot brass pole, flipped upside down, and spun around the pole as she slid to the bottom. The crowd cheered; several men threw money on the stage. As she exited, the deejay reminded the audience that "this lovely lady is available for a limited number of couch and lap dances" and that they should "hurry up and see the lap dance attendant for details and to buy a lap-dance ticket." Men pulled out their wallets and scurried anxiously over to the attendant, eagerly buying tickets as quickly as the attendant could sell them.

There were no other dancers on stage. I knew I was next. The deejay turned on the stage lights in a rapid-fire motion and cranked up the fog machine. He gave me the nod, reminded me that there was no touching, and said, "Break a leg." He blasted my music and announced my arrival. My knees trembled with excitement and nervousness as I descended the spiral staircase. Over the speakers, his voice boomed with authority, "And now, a new lady, taking the Divas stage for the first time . . . is the lovely, the luscious . . . " As I stepped onto the stage, I heard a customer say to the man next to him, "Wow, she's hot." "I am pretty hot," I said to myself. "I can do this." My night had begun.

After my audition, I went to have my picture taken and a copy of my id scanned. I was told I had lap dances waiting; I could go ahead and give the dances and work the rest of the evening. Then the manager would have to see if I would be allowed to work again. My first lap dance was an older man, sitting on his hands (as he had been instructed). A bouncer sat staring at us and giving me the raised eyebrow, asking nonverbally if everything was ok. I nodded that I was fine and read the sign above the couch: DO NOT TOUCH THE LADIES! DANCERS ARE ALLOWED TO TERMINATE DANCES AT ANY TIME.

I smiled as my customer told me how beautiful I was and how nice I smelled. He looked at me with awe. He was thoroughly enamored. "My God, You're beautiful." "You're perfect." "You're so amazing." We flirted as I lay on his chest and ran my fingers through his hair. When our time was up, the bouncer came over and escorted me back to the dressing room so that I could freshen up for my next customer, waiting in the crowd with his ticket.

By the end of the night, I had made a lot of money. I had danced and flirted all evening. I could still hear the flattery and applause and the sound of my favorite music blasting over the entire club. I put on my heels and danced in front of the mirror, imagining how the customers must have seen me. I was a goddess—a total sex kitten. When the club owner called the next day to let me know I was on the schedule, I squealed with delight. I was giddy. I had made the cut! I felt perfect and sexy, and I wanted more. After all, those men saw me that way. How could they all be wrong? I had had my ego stroked, and I was hooked. For the first time in my life, I had felt the power of physical beauty. There is a difference between feeling generally satisfied with your appearance and in feeling powerfully beautiful. The latter is exquisite. I looked in the mirror and soaked in that feeling. It was my first experience dancing, and it was one of the best nights of my life.

What made this experience so dramatically different from the incident described in the previous chapter? I took my clothes off in both establishments. I sat on men's laps in both establishments. I sold sex in both places. But *how* I sold sex varied greatly, with substantial effects on my perception of work. Whereas one club filled me with frustration and shame, the other seduced me with flattery and validation of attractiveness. What made the latter so attractive?

THE SOCIAL WORLD OF THE SHOW CLUB

In the following chapter I outline the second distinct type of social organization—the social world of the show club. I focus on the physical description of the club, the temporality of the interaction, the relative power, the primary method of money making, and the overall image promoted by the club management. I then discuss the impact of these structural characteristics on the meaning of dance and dancer subjective experiences working in show clubs. Specifically, I explore how the structural organization of show club affect commitment development and career continuation in exotic dance.

The following description outlines the structural features, individual perceptions and adjustments, and commitment development patterns of a typical show club. My description draws on my own experiences as well as my observations and interviews from a number of clubs, which I identify by the fictitious name *Babydoll's*. These establishments are characteristically similar to all clubs defined as "show clubs" by subjects and observational data.[1]

Babydoll's

Babydoll's is a large club located in a suburban location just outside a modern metropolis. It is a relatively new club, having recently undergone a highly advertised grand opening, complete with guest appearances of a famous pornographic film star. The club is featured on a billboard advertisement close to the interstate and promotes the image of a "gentlemen's club." Bouncers are required to wear tuxedos; valet parking is available.

The management is characterized as strict and aggressive; dancers are supervised at all times; rules are strictly enforced. All women who desire to work must call and schedule an audition; they must report their height, weight, and measurements before being considered for an audition. Auditions are held on the first Tuesday of the month for scheduled women only. They are held in private before the owner and manager. Those selected for employment are notified via telephone during the following two weeks.

Show clubs tend to be large in terms of physical layout, clientele, and dancer population. They are relatively clean and well

kept, and designed to be "classy." The upstairs section of Babydoll's consists of a large dressing room with a number of well-
lighted mirrors and several dressing tables. Upon being
announced, dancers descend, via a lighted staircase, to the stage
area, complete with advanced lighting equipment, top-quality
sound, and smoke effects. The stage area consists of a long main
stage and several smaller circular stages, all surrounded by black
leather seating. In the center of each stage area is a shiny twenty-
foot brass pole. Beyond the stage area, there is a lap-dance room,
supervised by an attendant.

The number of women working on any given night is very
consistent. On week nights, there are usually five to ten dancers
working before 9:00 p.m., ten to fifteen dancers working from
9:00 p.m. until closing time. On weekends, there are ten dancers
working prior to 9:00 p.m., and fifteen working between 9:00
p.m. and closing time.

The features associated with the "high-class atmosphere,"
including high cost of admission and valet parking, make fre-
quenting Babydoll's an expensive form of entertainment. All customers are required to pay a twenty-five dollar entrance fee. Both
alcoholic and nonalcoholic drinks are very expensive; domestic
beer ranges from five to eight dollars per bottle. Lap dances cost
between twenty and firty dollars. As a result, although Babydoll's
customers vary with regard to race and ages, the club predominantly attracts clientele from middle-class and upper socioeco-
nomic statuses. Customers are almost exclusively male, there
alone as well as in groups or pairs.

The customer population is relatively large; the typical show
club has more customers present than the social club but fewer
than the hustle clubs. There is a high turnover rate and few "regular" customers. Club management estimates that there are approximately 150 men there on any given weeknight; this estimate
approximately increases on weekends. However, the establishment
specializes in providing an atmosphere for "business lunches" and
professional socializing during early evening hours immediately
following work ("happy hour").

All dancers are required to pay a twenty-dollar stage fee per
night in order to work. Furthermore, dancers must "tip out" (pay)
each bouncer, the "doorman" (individual who greets and takes the
required cover charge from incoming customers), the attendant of

the lap-dance room, and the deejay. These tip outs involve a five-dollar minimum per person; dancers who refuse or forget to tip out receive a one-week suspension and are not permitted to work again until the tip out is paid.

The practices of the dancers at Babydoll's are highly regulated through both informal norm and formal club policy. Management enforces strict physical appearance requirements; dancers reported that one manager will not book dancers who appear to wear larger than a size four in women's clothing. Twice per week, dancers must attend an aerobics class and dance practice. Dancers who miss these sessions are not permitted to work during the following week. All dancers are required to purchase professional exotic dancer costumes. Lingerie from department stores and street clothes are not permitted.

Babydoll's has highly selective booking practices. Schedules are determined exclusively by management. Dancers may request to not work specific days, but these preferences are not guaranteed. Dancers who are the most attractive and sell the most dances are given first priority with regard to scheduling. Other dancers are then booked based on club needs.

Money making is based on a combination of stage performance and dance sales. Dancers are not permitted to "hustle" and are not allowed to be among the customers except during their time on stage. Instead, making money involves "putting on a good show"; this involves being attractive, being seductive or athletic, displaying impressive pole work, and wearing beautiful costumes. These acts are rewarded by customer tips. The idea is that if a dancer is the most entertaining or erotic, by being the most attractive, athletic, or having the best dancing ability, she will receive the most tips from customers on stage. In addition, the best performer is most likely to be selected by a customer who wishes to buy a lap dance.

When buying a lap dance, customers usually view all of the women and their performances and then select the dancer they find most appealing. Customers then go to the lap-dance room, pay the fee, and notify the attendant as to which dancer they would like. At that time, the attendant goes to the dressing room and informs the selected dancer. She then reports to the lap-dance room and performs the dance. Afterward, the dancer must return to the dressing room unless the customer purchases another dance.

ADJUSTING TO THE WORLD OF THE SHOW CLUB

All clubs that dancers identified as show clubs share similar structural characteristics and subsequent adjustment and commitment development patterns as Babydoll's. The social organization of the show club is characterized as highly selective, competitive, and self-oriented among dancers.

Rather than relying on aggressive sales, the environment of the show club is one of passive selection. Using this technique, the show club takes on a "beauty pageant" atmosphere, in which dancers vie for management approval in order to work and customer approval in order to make money. Thus, this environment is characterized by asymmetrical power relations, in that dancers are successful only to the extent that they please customers and management.

In show clubs, owners and management are primarily focused on maintaining the high standards and professional atmosphere of the establishment. This is big business; they have little time for or interest in developing relationships with individual dancers. Subsequently, interactions between dancers and management are typically detached and professional. The highly selective hiring process generates an atmosphere in which women believe they are lucky to have been selected; they subsequently continue striving to be the best in order to keep their jobs.

The use of dance sales and stage tipping as the main method of making money acts so that dancers compete among each other for their economic livelihood. However, the business atmosphere and pageantlike environment discourage aggressive behavior against one's fellow dancers. In many show clubs, there are written and strongly enforced rules stating a zero-tolerance policy for antagonistic behaviors; prohibited conduct includes name calling, stealing, physical or verbal fighting, or tampering with property of other dancers. Dancers are regularly reminded by management that they are "entertainers" and that they should conduct themselves in a detached, "professional" manner. Thus, there are both formal and informal norms that discourage both hostility and personal involvement among dancers.

Moreover, it is very difficult to make a competitor less beautiful or affect her dancing abilities. Accordingly, although there is considerable competition among dancers, the competition is nonhostile. Because being the most beautiful or best dancer is the overall goal promoted by the club environment, and consequently the best way of making money, dancers focus their energies on meeting this goal. Rather than externally focusing hostility on competitors, dancers are better served to center their energies on being better competitors themselves. That is, dancers must try to improve themselves to compete with their fellow dancers. Each dancer must make herself thinner, prettier, more skilled, and so on. As a result, dancing at a show club is highly self-oriented.

Self-orientation and professionalism function so that interpersonal interactions with fellow dancers are often limited to topics related to self-improvement. Other dancers are competition, and dancers act as individual performers to be rated by potential clients. However, in contrast to the aggressive, "dog-eat-dog" behavior of the hustle club, dancers do not project hostility toward another dancer for being selected for a lap dance. Rather, not being chosen is a reflection of an individual dancer's failure to be the most appealing. As one dancer explains: "It's a matter of self-esteem. When a girl gets a dance, Pete [the lap-dance attendant] comes up [to the dressing room] and tells her, but it's in front of everyone. So we all know who's selling dances and who's not. You can see the other girls react, even though they don't say anything. We all wanna be the best, the most popular, sell the most [dances]. So a girl feels good when she gets a dance 'cuz she knows she's pretty . . . The guys like her" (Lacy, twenty-six, danced four years).

Showcasing

Other organizational elements emphasize the pageantlike nature of dancing at the show club. One of the most notable features is a practice called showcasing, a system instituted exclusively at show establishments.[2] Showcasing essentially involves featuring all dancers on stage simultaneously; in effect, presenting them for approval before the customers. Much like a "formal wear" portion of a beauty contest, every dancer is required to dress in an evening gown. During this time, dancers form a single-file line on stage and then proceed to walk through the crowd. While the dancers are being presented, lap dances are sold at discount rates. Customers are persuaded to "pick your favorite lady."

The act of showcasing typifies what it means to be a dancer at a show club. Observations of behavior prior to and during showcasing reveal that, to dancers, participation in showcasing, and in show clubs more generally, is primarily oriented with validation. Although almost all dancers eventually are selected for a dance during this time, dancers take great pride in being one of the first selected by a customer. Dancing for these women, just like dancers in the hustle club, is competitive. However, unlike the money-centered focus of the hustle club dancers, show club dancers are not competing as much for money. Rather, they are competing for affirmation.

Showcasing involves the sale of only one lap dance per dancer, and nearly all dancers usually receive a dance. In other words, all dancers typically make the same amount of money. Yet the time immediately preceding showcasing is full of activity. The tone is anxious, with women moving hurriedly and constantly readjusting their appearance. Observations and dancer interviews indicate that most dancers exert a considerable amount of time and energy, carefully selecting which evening gown to wear, touching up makeup, and restyling hair throughout the evening; these behaviors were particularly apparent in preparation for showcasing.

The nervousness and effort experienced in anticipation of this event make obvious that dancers internalize club norms regarding what it means to be a dancer. Although money is important, dancers are particularly determined to strive for superiority or validation of their attractiveness. Selling a dance or making money on stage seems to take on meaning beyond simple financial benefit. In the show club, the customers assume the role of judges, with dancers as contestants; subsequently, the goal of the dancers is not only making money but also in being "picked." Thus, not selling a dance (such as during showcasing) is perceived by dancers as individual failure. Being one of the last dancers selected is described as a particularly upsetting event by dancers: "Yeah, you're just standing around hoping you get picked and looking like a loser" (Lacy). "I'm just walking around, trying not to look like it bothers me, putting on a fake smile like it's not humiliating. And then some dude will finally take you, 'cuz you're like one of the only ones left" (Juliet, twenty-five).

These quotes illustrate how dancers' personal stake in being preferred by customers is perceived not only in relation to making money but to being validated as well. Whereas hustle club dancers lament the loss of a sale in terms of financial loss, and project frustrations outward (toward other dancers or customers), show club dancers internalize this loss. Much like the runners-up in a pageant, women who are not preferred by customers perceived this experience in terms of humiliation and individual inadequacy.

Dancers are aware that there are a number of other women who did not get hired and would eagerly take their jobs. Accordingly, they feel little bargaining power in relation to management expectations. Instead, they focus their energies on issues in which they do have power. That is, because they have little power to control the conditions in which they work, they focus their efforts internally by modifying themselves to meet or exceed these conditions. They cannot change the standards, yet they can change *themselves* in order to conform to the beauty or performance expectations and club norms.

How do the expectations of dancers at show clubs impact thier lives? It seems that dancers adapt to the culturally proscribed means for acceptance and admiration in the show club world by continually striving to be thinner, prettier, sexier, and better. My observations revealed that, despite their extreme beauty, these women often appeared insecure. What may have initially felt empowering frequently developed into obsession: they became "affirmation addicts." Dancers became fixated on their "flaws" and often seemed absorbed with self-improvement. During my interviews and my time in show clubs, I found women constantly criticizing their faces, bodies, costumes, and dance moves—perpetually seeking confirmation among their peers. Dancers regularly compared themselves to their coworkers and reported constantly trying to self-improve. Responses indicated that dancers typically perceived continual self-scrutiny as beneficial. Self-improvements were motivated by the anticipation of increased adoration and more money from their clientele.

Starri, a slender brunette, discussed her adaptations to the show club: "Well, I had to really cut back on what I ate. I saw all those girls up there, and they had, like, perfect bodies—zero fat. So, I didn't want to go up [on stage] after girls like that. I mean, I'm tall, so I try to play that up, 'cuz some guys like tall girls. And, so, I really think I look taller when I'm skinnier too. And I'm thinking about going blonde. The blonde girls make more money. Men think blondes are sexier."

Tabitha, a dancer for five years, stated, "I totally need a boob job. The girls with big tits make better money. And all the costumes look better when you have big boobs. So, I'm saving up. I hate my little breasts. I need really big ones. I can't wait. If I could get them tomorrow, I would. I can't stand not having boobs. I have the smallest breasts in here."

One dancer's statements exemplify the internally focused adjustment strategy in response to strictly enforced beauty standards: "My audition was fine. But Kris [the manager] just told me I was too fat. They only want really skinny girls. I'd be the fattest one there. He said if I lost fifteen or twenty pounds and came back and auditioned again that they might put me up on stage. So now I'm fucking dietin' like a maniac" (Kyra, twenty-two, danced three times).

Summer describes the similar experience of a fellow dancer: "Vega is on suspension. Apparently Lee [the club manager and owner's son] told her she needed to tone up. She's pretty sexy and sold enough dances, but she's put on a little weight lately. Not like she's fat or anything. But Lee told her she needed to go to the gym and work out more . . . She's not fat, but not toned enough. So, she'll probably come back later."

These quotes demonstrate how, in order to meet the expectations of clubs, dancers focus their energies internally. In other words, rather than expend their efforts toward manipulating customers and management, they must manipulate themselves in order to meet standards externally imposed upon them. The club atmosphere operates so that dancers take on the roles of contestants, each aspiring to be regarded favorably by management and clients.

Within this environment, women are forced to set aside personal preferences in favor of club demands on their physical attractiveness and abilities. In order to be "picked," dancers then must maintain the high standards of beauty, stage performance, and physical ability upon which they will be judged. As mentioned earlir, one manager proudly stated that he never hired women who wore bigger than size four clothing. Similarly, during my observations of the backstage behavior and dialogue of dancers in the dressing room, I overheard the following statements:

> "I was told that I'd need to get breast implants if I wanted
> to keep working here."

"I am way too pasty white to be working. I have got to start tanning again. It just dries my skin out so badly. But that's it. I've just got to start going."

"Look at my ass! I'm so fat. I've put on like three pounds in the last month! It's water, but I still look awful."

"Oh, no! Never drink sodas! They make you bloated, and it's harder to suck in your stomach on stage. I haven't had even a diet soda in forever, but I've noticed a difference."

Negotiating the world of the show club involves a subjugation of the actual self in favor of a self that is competitive in this economically and admiration-motivated environment. In adjusting to the pageantlike atmosphere, women construct, and then subsequently strive to attain, an "ideal" identity. That is, they create a fantasy image of what they perceive their customers desire. In doing so, show club dancers operate as actors or performers, playing a role before an audience. Becoming a client's "fantasy" often requires a great deal of physical and financial effort.

One adjustment of dancers to the beauty-pageant atmosphere of the show club involves placing particular emphasis on performance-related behavior and objects. Most women in show clubs reported spending a large amount of time to develop and practice routines; many also stated that they exerted substantial energy learning how to dance and do "pole work" (artistic use of a pole, present on many club stages, during an erotic performance). "No one can do some of the shit I do up there. I been busting my ass to figure it out, practicing 'til I was black and blue. But I got some cool shit" (Tori, twenty-seven, danced five years). "Sasha's fantastic. I can't believe some of the things she can do with her body. It's unbelievable. Sometime I just sit and watch her flip around and shit. She's amazing" (Madison, twenty-eight, danced three years).

Although the social organization of the show clubs creates asymmetrical power relations in favor of management, dancers do exhibit power in negotiations with customers. That is, although women perceive that they can be easily replaced by management, the portrayal of dancers as "goddesses" as evidenced by club practices creates a perception of power over customers among dancers.

The performance atmosphere of the club and club practices individualizes dancers.

Such practices include the announcement of each dancer prior to appearing on stage, dancer selection of her own music, the high placement of the stage, and the limited, highly monitored customer contact with dancers. These practices create the image that dancers are "goddesses"; they are, in effect, "above" the customers. By meeting the high expectations of the club, dancers have become the ideal. As a consequence, on a given night, in negotiations with customers, dancers become irreplaceable, while patrons become replaceable. Because they have become what they believe every man wants, they are to be adored and admired. "I get told how gorgeous I am all night. There's nothing wrong with that. And yeah, they have to pay me. They have to pay me for my attention. They work hard all week to make money and then hand it all over to me on a Saturday night. *It's not demeaning to me; it's demeaning to them.* They give me money 'cuz that's all they have to give" (Erica, twenty-five, danced three years).

Club policies both create an atmosphere in which dancers have little power relative to management and simultaneously promote the image of dancers as goddesses to customers. In response, dancers feel both powerful and individually identified with their work. Thus, the aspiration for perfection common among participants in show clubs creates an environment in which dancers are both controlled and controlling. Although they are common when negotiating with management, they are individual performers when they are on stage and interacting with clients.

The opportunity to become individually identified with participating in a course of action is evidenced by the importance among show club dancers of putting on their best (unique) performance. This importance is emphasized by informal dancer norms regarding dancing and pole work. Dancers exert a significant amount of effort to develop unique individual routines and abilities; as a consequence, they become very protective of these practices. Although dancers are not openly hostile, there is a considerable amount of disdain among them for coworkers who "copy." Most show club dancers reported that fellow dancers are very protective of their skills, refusing to teach other dancers how to do pole work or dance in a particular way: "I really enjoy it. I want to learn how to do pole work, but you gotta be careful not to do something some other girl's already doing. She'll get pissed if she thinks you might be stealing her move. It makes things real uncomfortable" (Camille, twenty-two, danced six months).

In addition to the development of dancing and pole abilities, dancers at show clubs also utilize clothing to enhance their presentation. Hustle club dancers are most often naked or typically wear one costume throughout the night. In contrast, show club women reported spending a large amount of money on expensive professional costumes and accessories. Many also indicated that they had had costumes designed and custom made. Such costumes varied in price; however, many dancers had purchased outfits costing as much as two hundred dollars each. A dancer who reports having worked at a show club for approximately three years, advises: "Pretty much all of your money in the beginning goes to costumes. You just can't go down on the stage in your house drawers [conventional underwear]. Go to a real exotic clothing store. All real stripper costumes cost a lot. So, I will usually tell a new girl that she should bust her butt everyday to make as much as she can and put it all toward getting costumes and platforms [expensive shoes worn almost exclusively by dancers, typically having five- or six-inch platform soles and spike heels, believed by dancers to accentuate the legs and buttocks]. Just plan on spending it that way."

In addition, show club dancers were more likely to report spending money on expensive makeup, tanning, gym memberships and hair and nail salons. Furthermore, undergoing plastic surgery was a common practice among dancers at show clubs. As one dancer explains, "Honey, we've all had something done. Me, I had my eyes done. And, obviously, we all have boob jobs. If a girl says she hasn't had something done, she's lying. There's no way" (Chel, twenty-nine, danced five years).

One dancer reported having had breast augmentation surgery twice; another reported having undergone breast augmentation twice and planning another (in order to repair a broken silicone implant).

Moreover, many dancers who had not undergone cosmetic surgery indicated that they would do so if they could afford it. These statements point out the substantial amount of effort dancers expend in order to be successful in show clubs. Dancers often reported similar "body-conscious" behaviors, such as exercising excessively and extreme dieting; many professed that such practices are essential in order to attain or maintain a "perfect" physique.

Rachel's Story

The following passage is from an interview with Rachel, a twenty-five-year-old dancer in a show club. Her story and interview responses are characteristic of study participants currently or previously involved in show club dancing. Like Brianna, Rachel also began dancing shortly after high school. Having been raised by her single father after the death of her mother while Rachel was an infant, she describes her childhood as "normal. My dad worked, and I stayed with my grandparents during the day. No big issues. Just normal teenager stuff, running around getting into trouble. But nothing big." Rachel has a young daughter. She has been dancing between five and six years, usually working three nights per week. She has recently undergone breast augmentation surgery. Like other dancers, Rachel stated that although originally it was upsetting, she is now very happy to have had her child so young, "when my body could bounce back, and you could not really tell I've had a kid." She describes her experience dancing:

> I started dancing right after high school. I had a baby my senior year and was working at McDonald's. I never looked like this [referring to her current attractiveness]. I'd heard about this club in town . . . [S]ome guys I knew and was friends with talked about it . . . so one night after work I went down there, just to see. I saw all these women up there, looking gorgeous, and I thought, "I could do that." I'm a complete attention whore. So I got fixed up and went back. I got on that stage, and that was it . . . I never really went back [to her previous employer] . . .
>
> M: Have you ever thought about quitting? What do you think you'd do if you quit?
>
> Yeah sure. I was dating this guy once, and he was giving me a hard time about it. I live with my dad, and I knew it was bothering him . . . so I quit for a while and starting working at [an expensive department store], working at the makeup counter, and went to school for cosmetology. That's been really helpful as a dancer . . . I know how to really do hair and makeup. It was fine, but I really didn't make a whole lot. So I went back to dancing and have been doing this ever since . . . I just can't find anything else I like doing as much. My dad and my new

man give me a hard time, but I love dancing. I like dressing up and performing. I like getting paid to look good
and dance ... the stage and the lights ... What else
would I do?

No other job is like this. I love what I do. I mean,
especially now that I have my boobs. I hated being so
skinny in high school. But it's great now, because guys
actually like skinny dancers, as long as they have breasts.
And I have a huge collection of gorgeous costumes. I love
dancing when I get a new costume. I can't wait until my
next set to wear it. And, if I get a new CD or learn a new
pole trick, I can't wait to get up there. Sometimes I can't
wait to get to work. I mean, I'll wake up in the afternoon,
work out, go tanning, get my dance bag ready ...
y'know, organize my costumes and plan my sets. That
usually gets me in the mood to work ... By the time I get
my dance bag packed, get my makeup on, and fix my
hair, I am actually pretty happy going in to work. I mean,
it's hard work, and I get exhausted, especially by the end
of the night. I have good nights and bad nights, but so do
people at other jobs. Everyone gets tired; everyone has
nights when they'd rather be at home. Who really wants
to work? But if you have to work, it's not a bad gig. I
think about how most people feel going in to work:
they're fuckin' miserable. That sucks. But me, I've slept
in, gotten laid, look hot, and feel sexy; I want to strut my
stuff. So work ain't such a big deal for me!

M: What about your man ... how do you deal with
that?

I pretty much tell every guy I've ever been with that
this is what I do and who I am ... deal. I'm a dancer, and
a damn good one. To be honest, I'm good at this and
really not good at anything else! And I'm not interested in
anything else. I'm not quitting.

Rachel's narrative illustrates how dancer perceptions and
negotiation strategies are influenced by the social organization of
the show club. Her work atmosphere is performance and beauty
oriented. To be successful at this type of club requires a dancer to
be her most glamorous and beautiful. In response to these contextual conditions, Rachel then adjusts her behavior to achieve and

maintain the expectations of her environment. Her success in the show club subsequently becomes a source of professional pride and a validation of her good looks. That is, this environment provides her the opportunity to develop personal commitment in that being a "successful" dancer has become both *satisfying* and a source of *personal identity*.

5

DANCING AT THE SOCIAL CLUB

was home on a Saturday afternoon when Haylee called. We had met while working at Divas. I had given her my number in hopes of getting an interview. Divas had been closed for remodeling for more than a month, with no signs of reopening anytime soon. I had started looking for a new club in which to work during the interim. Haylee stated that she had found Tom's, a club that was not far away. "They're short of girls here, since one of the girls is pregnant and won't be working for a while. Dina [the manager] asked if I knew anyone that was good and would fit in. No bullshit. So I thought about you. You need a club. This place is pretty cool. Laid back. You don't make much, but it's a lot of fun. You should come out. Even if you don't like it, you'll come out and have a few drinks. It'll be fun." I was not thrilled about the idea of not making much money, but I jumped at the opportunity to get to dance and check out a new club. I also suspected that, since the club wasn't busy, we would be able to actually have some interview time.

As I walked into Tom's, I spotted Haylee sitting at the bar, playing an electronic game machine with a customer. She waved me over enthusiastically. "This is Chris. He's a regular around here." Chris shook my hand and agreed that "he'd been coming to this place forever." He stated that he "knew everyone around here." He bought me a drink as I joined in their game. Afterward, Haylee showed me around and introduced me to all the other regulars: Frank, the retired attorney, Bob, the truck driver, Keith, who works at the local TV station. We then went to meet Dina, the club manager. Dina smiled and asked if I could be ready to go on

stage in twenty minutes. "Will that be enough time? Or would
later be better? Haylee, you be sure to tell her about how it
works—the rules and all. I know you said she was cool. So just let
her know what to do."

I was led into the cramped, smoky dressing room, where four
dancers were getting ready for the evening and gossiping. Haylee
introduced me, and each of the women said hello. "My God!
You've got great hair," Amber exclaimed. "Thanks. But I wish it
was straight like yours, instead of this curly mess." I quickly became
involved in the group discussion. During the course of the evening,
we talked about the events at the club the previous night, the lives
of each of the regular customers, opinions about the new local chain
restaurant opening in town, Amber's boyfriend (who apparently
was "no good" and had been in the club a few nights ago), a
dancer's son's problems at school and her parent-teacher conference,
and various club gossip. "Do you shoot pool? Because Keith, the
dark-haired guy out there, and I are on this pool league, and I could
use some practice." "How far did you drive to get here? If you start
working here regularly, maybe we could car pool."

After dressing, I went to the deejay booth. The sound and
light system was simple, with a small, six-disc CD player used to
program songs. There was basic lighting; no smoke machine or
strobe. Although the club had a number of house CDs, the deejay
invited me to look through his private CD collection, because the
"house collection is pretty limited." As I flipped through the
pages, a customer went out to his truck. He returned with his own
CD case, to give me more choices.

As Bill announced my turn over the microphone, I crossed
paths with the dancer on before me (later identified as Andrea).
She wished me good luck and told me she would come back out to
cheer me on after she got dressed. Haylee and Chris got up from
the bar and tapped several of the regular customers on the shoul-
der. They all came down to sit at the stage. As I danced, each one
politely placed a dollar in my hand. One customer, pleased with
my song selection, gave me "a dollar for you, and a dollar for
your music. Good songs!" My night had begun.

I looked over at the two men shooting pool across from the
stage. I waved to them to get their attention. One nodded, took a
dollar from his wallet and got a dollar from his companion. He
came over and placed them on the rail of the stage. "Good job,"
he stated, as he went back to focusing on his game.

During the middle of my set, I walked over to Andrea and began chatting. Chris and Keith were both singing along with my music. Frank waved over from the far end of the bar and gave me a "thumbs up." He then signaled with his hand and mouthed, "Do you want a drink?" Other customers introduced themselves and shook my hand as I approached them on stage.

At the end of the night, I sat in a plastic lawn chair in the dressing room, finishing a gin and tonic and counting my money. Haylee and Andrea came in to ask if I was going to breakfast. So I went to breakfast with the club waitress, the deejay, three dancers, and four regular customers. We took up the corner of the restaurant and were almost the only patrons. The waitress at the restaurant knew everyone but me by name. We stayed up drinking coffee and talking until 4:00 a.m. I exchanged numbers with Bill and Andrea, and Keith offered to burn me a CD of some of my favorite songs. We exchanged adieus as I waved and drove out of the parking lot: "See you next week." "Be careful driving home." "It was great to meet you."

I had worked an entire evening and had only made a little over two hundred dollars. I danced there regularly for the next three years. I cried the night I finally quit.

Whereas some clubs have large and constantly changing populations in terms of dancers, customers, and staff, other clubs tend to have roughly the same smaller group of customers, dancers, and other employees time after time. In the following paragraphs I present the social world of the "social club." I outline the properties of the world of social club dancing, based on interview responses and observational data. I focus on physical descriptions of clubs, temporality of interactions, relative power, method of money making, and overall image promoted by management. I then discuss the relationship between these structural characteristics and career persistence. Specifically, I explain how the organizational features of the social club affect dancers' perceptions of work and attitudes toward fellow dancers, customers, and management, and subsequent commitment formation.

THE SOCIAL WORLD OF THE SOCIAL CLUB

The following description outlines the structural features, individual perceptions and adjustments, and commitment development patterns of a typical social club. Although I present the description as that of one club, which I identify by the fictitious name *Fantasy*, this club is a composite of a number of clubs characteristically similar to all clubs defined as "social clubs" by subjects and observational data.

Fantasy

Fantasy is a club in the relatively small urban area of Jonston. Once a busy city with thriving railroad industry and mills, Jonston has long been in a state of economic decline, with the exception of growth in food and service industries. The club is very small, consisting primarily of one large bar area and a single, limited stage area; the stage usually features only one dancer at a time. There is one small dressing room, with only two chairs, used primarily to hold the dancers' coats and purses during the night. The club has two pool tables and a few video games. Notably, there are no champagne or lap-dance areas.

Subsequently, there is little ability for the club or the dancers to make large sums of money through the sale of sexual arousal. Instead, the club is characterized by customers and staff, as primarily a local bar, incorporating the dancers as part of the "good time" atmosphere. For the club, the primary method of making money is through bar sales. The establishment stocks a full bar and features low-price drink specials. The dancers do not sell drinks and make no profit from alcohol sales.

For the dancers, the primary method of making money is through tipping on stage, which, due to the relatively small, working-class clientele, tends to be rather limited. To compensate for the lower money-making ability, the club pays each dancer five dollars per set (defined unit of time, ranging from fifteen to twenty minutes on stage) per night. Social club dancers change costumes a few times per night; their costumes are likely to consist of "street clothes" and department store lingerie, as well as professional dancewear.

Al, a local biker and native of Jonston, has been the owner of Fantasy for more than fifteen years. In addition to the owner, the management, bartenders, and deejay have remained unchanged as well. For example, Dina, the head bartender and manager, has been working there since Al purchased the establishment. Similarly, the barmaid, Lyn, has been working at Fantasy for more than ten years.

In addition to club staff, the dancer population is also small and stable. The club usually averages between three and five dancers on a weeknight and typically features five or six dancers on a weekend. Usually, dancers make their schedules one week in advance; they work a regular, posted schedule. The dancer turnover rate is very low. Many of the dancers have been employed at Fantasy for years and most have worked the same three to five nights per week each week for several years. Most dancers are women from the town of Jonston or the immediately surrounding areas.

Dancers characterize the clientele as similar to "people at a regular redneck bar." The clients are predominantly white, blue-collar males, ranging from their late twenties to upper sixties. The club consists primarily of repeat customers, individuals who patronize the establishment regularly over extended periods of time. Such attendance patterns range from daily to every other week. Many of the clients have been coming to this bar since its establishment fifteen years ago.

ADJUSTING TO THE WORLD OF THE SOCIAL CLUB

All clubs that dancers identified as primarily social clubs share similar structural characteristics and subsequent adjustment and commitment development patterns as Fantasy. The structural organization of the social club is characterized as small, stable, and relatively isolated. As a consequence, customers, dancers, and owners must interact on a regular, long-term basis.

The limited amount of alternative places to dance as well as available dancers fostered symmetrical power relations. Club owners are more willing to negotiate with dancers both because owners have more frequent contact and opportunity to get to know their employees and because dancers are less expendable. In a dispute, an owner must be willing to make concessions to a dancer simply because he needs enough dancers for the club to operate, and there might be few or no other dancers available. In turn, dancers are more willing to cooperate with management because they have more regular contact and have fewer other clubs available for employment.

That is, if a woman in this area wants to dance without traveling a great distance, she must dance in this club. This balance of power and long-term relationship orientation creates the context in which women feel that they have an influence in club dynamics. Many women reported that their concerns are taken into account by management; none indicated that management regarded them as expendable or replaceable.

The use of bar sales as management's primary method of making money deemphasizes the need for competition and promotes a cooperative atmosphere. For dancers, there are no lap dances or champagne rooms to sell. Moneymaking is limited to onstage tipping, although many women reported that they consider receiving free drinks purchased by customers as part of their financial incentive.

For dancers, working at a social club is not extremely profitable. These clubs ranked lowest when compared to hustle and show clubs in terms of money-making potential. Almost all of the social club dancers reported that a "very good" night was around $100 to $150. Most women worked three to four nights per week. Because there is little money to be made and a very limited way of making it, there is little competition, as women feel no need to "hustle" customers.

Rather than having no enforcement of rules, as in the hustle clubs, social clubs are characterized by a combination of dancer self-governance and involved management. In contrast to dancer perceptions of lawlessness and corresponding "dog-eat-dog" adjustment to the hustle club, the social club exhibits an established, disciplined social order of relatively harmonious relations that is perpetuated by dancer regulation. That is, upon entering the club environment, new dancers are "taken under the wing" of the other dancers. The club owner and bar manager also frequently interact with the dancers and check in on how the dancers are getting along and how new dancers are adjusting to the club. The purpose of management is primarily to "maintain the peace," typically intervening if a dispute arises or issues are unable to be resolved. As Savannah, who danced at Fantasy exclusively for more than four years, explained:

> Al is there all the time. He's pretty laid back. He's there if we have a problem, but he's usually pretty hands-off. But that's fine, 'cuz we usually don't really need him to do

much: we handle things ourselves. If a girl's doing something, like illegal or something, we'll tell her about it and
ask her to straighten up. I mean, it's all our jobs if she's
doin' shit. She gets busted for sucking dick, and we all get
fined. Even if she doesn't get caught, then the guy might
start expecting stuff from other girls. So we don't let that
go on. We're not mean to her or anything, for all we
know she could be really hard up [in need of money] and
desperate. But one of us will tell her that we know what
she's doin' and that's not cool here . . . We wanna make
sure that we're all doing the same thing. Let's just all
agree to not do that shit . . . Then if it keeps up, we'll go
to Al, and he'll fire her . . . Al doesn't put up with any cat-
tiness or bitching. We all get along here, and if a girl is
causing trouble, gossiping or some shit, and all of us are
having a problem with the same girl, he'll quit booking
her . . . He'll even ban a customer who's being difficult. If
a guy is being rude to the girls, trying to touch 'em or getting obnoxious, we'll tell Al or Dina. Al will kick him out
and not let him come back.

Sierra, a dancer with more than five years of experience at a
social club, stated that having an informal policy of dancer self-
regulation is the most effective way of indoctrinating new dancers.
She explained:

Dancers need to help other dancers; that's the quickest
way to learn. It helps her adjust quicker. Whenever we get
a new girl, one of us, usually me or Andrea, will show her
the ropes. If she doesn't know how to work the music or
how to run a set [plan a sequence of events on stage, such
as at what point she should disrobe], we tell how to do it.
Often a girl who's never danced doesn't know how to
take tips [accept money on stage]. Or a girl who's danced
somewhere else doesn't know the specifics about how it
works here . . . like whether she can take money with her
tits [accepting money by having the customers place the
dollars in the cleavage between her breasts] or if she can
flash [move her g-string to the side without removing it in
order to temporarily reveal her genitals] or not and we'll
tell her what we do here . . . I know what it's like to be in

a new place where you don't know anyone or what you're expected to do. We've all been there. So we try to help out the new girl, tell her the written rules and then the practical stuff.

M: What do you mean by the practical stuff?

How things really go on or some tricks of the trade. Like, the law and the house rules say that we can't show our nipples and that all of the genital area must be covered . . . so we'll tell her that most of us just put stickers over our nipples rather than buying real pasties that never stay on and look awful. And we'll tell her that her thong can't be see-through or mesh. That's what the written rules actually amount to. Or we'll tell her about this or that customer.

M: What about this or that customer?

Oh, things like, if Bob comes in, go over and say hi . . . he gives all of us twenty dollars. Or, when you dance for Tim, look him in the eye, 'cuz he gets uncomfortable looking at your body; he likes to look you in the eye. Or, be extra nice to Ken; his wife just left him and he's been really depressed.

These interview excerpts demonstrate the advisory roles dancers take in the socialization of new dancers. In effect, dancers feel responsible for the maintenance and enforcement of club informal and formal norms. When a new dancer enters the club environment, those currently working there feel compelled to "show her the logistical ropes," including telling her "what the written rules really amount to" as well as provide her with practical advice (including some "tricks of the trade") that encourage her likelihood of success. The act of "taking in" new dancers demonstrates how dancers assume responsibility for club socialization.

Such cooperative and supportive initiation processes among dancers assimilate new dancers into the informal culture and inform new dancers about the overall positive image of the club. Contrary to the image of the dancer as competition, the informal practices of the social club create the image of the dancer as a congenial team member.

Whereas being successful in a hustle club requires women to be good con artists, being successful at a typical social club requires women to establish and maintain mutually respectful social relationships.

Club Initiation

The process of fellow dancer socialization promotes friendly relations among dancers as older dancers become "mentors" to new dancers, and new dancers often appreciate having this guidance and acceptance. Dancers who are currently employed at a social club frequently enlist the help of friends, coworkers at other jobs, and acquaintances to meet the needs of the club. As a result, the majority of social club dancers indicated that they knew their coworkers well and worked with each other more frequently. Many began their careers in dance through their friendships with women who were already involved in dancing. "We all get along here. I started dancing here because my friend Tina said they really needed girls here. I was really nervous, but she was very encouraging. And Bruce [the owner], John [the deejay], and her cheered me on. Later my friend Skye found out that I did it and said she was interested, so I brought her along" (Cricket, twenty-four, danced two years).

In addition to frequent reporting of social club initiation processes in dancers' interviews, I was present during the first appearance of several of the dancers at clubs characteristically similar to Fantasy. The following paragraphs describe a typical initiation process of a dancer at a social club:

> Upon her arrival, Tasha was introduced to all of the customers and management staff at the bar by Savannah (a friend who was already employed at Fantasy). Then, Celine, another dancer with no prior relation to Tasha, showed Tasha how to program her music while Savannah explained the rules and etiquette regarding dancing on stage. A regular customer introduced himself once more and bought Tasha a drink while a member of the bar staff showed her around the club, then directing her to the dressing room. In the dressing room, another dancer, who also had no prior relation to Tasha, helped her decide which outfit she should wear on stage. As Tasha prepared to go on stage, Celine told her, "Relax, it's no

big deal. You're going to do great. Just don't forget to take off your top!"

The deejay introduced Tasha; he informed the crowd that this was her first time ever dancing, so they should be really nice to her. While Tasha was dancing, Savannah went around the bar and recruited several regular customers to come over to the stage with her to "cheer Tasha on." Both Savannah and Celine sat with a number of the customers and other dancers and provided encouragement and applause. Several dancers proceeded to tip Tasha, using their own previously acquired tips. Afterward, the deejay told Tasha she "did real good" over the microphone. Everyone, including Al, Dinah, the other dancers, and the customers, applauded. Savannah met Tasha off stage with another drink, purchased with Savannah's own money, and told her she was "proud of her." Then a regular customer shook her hand and asked her if she wanted to shoot a game of pool.

Observations and interviews suggest that such initiation experiences are typical of social club establishments. Furthermore, because of the collegial nature of the experience, dancers in social clubs consistently regarded social clubs, other dancers, and dancing in general as more positive. I spoke with Tasha immediately after her club debut:

M: Well, how'd it feel being there?

It was awesome. Savannah had been telling me how fun it was working here, and I had always wanted to try it. I was terrified. I thought there was no way I was going to be able to do it—dance topless in front of strangers— but it was fun! I had a great time. I wish I'd done it sooner. Everyone was so nice. It's a real laid-back place where people just go to cut loose and have a good time. I'm from a blue-collar family, so I fit right in.

M: Did you feel degraded?

No way. It was just fun. It was more about me being free and open with myself and my body and sexuality. I mean, I was standing up there practically naked and cutting loose and having fun. One thing that really got to me was something Savannah said. When I was done, she started cheering and clapping and told me "I'm proud of you." I dunno, but I guess I needed that. That was the perfect thing to say. I wasn't degraded and had nothing to be ashamed of—including my body. I was proud of myself—that I could just get up there and be myself—no clothes to hide behind. After that, I was on a "high" all night.

A five-month follow-up interview with Tasha revealed that she is now a regular dancer at Fantasy. She usually works between one and three nights per week, and plans on working there full time after completing college next semester.

This interview excerpt demonstrates how, upon entering the environment, new dancers receive both encouragement and instruction on the "how-tos" of dancing. In addition to already having a friend provide support and instruction, Tasha received assistance and encouragement from fellow dancers upon entering the club atmosphere. Fellow dancers allayed her anxiety, applauded her performance, and provided a welcome environment for her to begin her participation. By being both recruited by those in their preexisting social network and socialized into the club atmosphere in a cooperative manner, dancers regard their coworkers positively. Fellow dancers have then defined themselves to new dancers as helpful and instrumental in the new dancer's socialization.

Nadia's Story

The following paragraphs are taken from an in-depth interview with Nadia, a twenty-seven-year-old respondent who danced in a social club for more than five years. Her story and interview responses are characteristic of study participants currently or previously working in social clubs. Although she stated that she had "retired," she reported still dancing "every now and then . . . a night every week or so."

I had to quit Fantasy, though I still want to work there. I am just too outta shape, and Eli [her boyfriend] wanted me to quit. I still see a bunch of the guys around town though. They keep asking about when I'm coming back. So I think I'll still have to work a night or two every now and then for a while longer. I just can't go full time anymore . . .

I started dancing there a long time ago. I was hard up for money, and . . . well . . . Diva got me into it actually. She brought me in one night to shoot pool and have a drink with her while she was workin' . . . And I realized that it was not at all like I thought it was going to be. I had some drinks and then figured, why not? I loved it immediately. I'm not the most attractive, but I play good music that the guys like and danced and shot pool. So now I have my regular customers who ask about me.

M: What are you doing, now that you've retired?

I work for a painting company, painting apartments. I make a lot more steady money now. It's guaranteed, unlike stripping money. And it's a check, not cash that I spend without thinkin'. But it's only a couple days a week. And Eli works at night. So when I'm not at Fantasy's I'm at home, sittin' there, with nothing to do.

M: Are there people who are disappointed that you're not there?

Oh yeah. I talked with Sierra just the other day. She says the guys were asking about me . . . and she said it was boring without me there. She and I are like partners in crime. Her man doesn't want her dancing either, so she has to sneak around and go there when he's not around. She said next time she's gonna stop by and pick me up, so we can work together. I miss doing that. We had a hell of a good time having a drink, shooting pool, and dancing. We'd even get on the stage together sometimes . . . She'd be on stage, and I'd be teasing her, then she'd just grab my arm and pull me on stage with her, and we'd dance our asses off, high-fiving and shit, smacking each other's asses, hamming it up.

Nadia's story is consistent with experiences frequently reported by dancers at social club establishments. It illustrates how the social organization of the hustle club influences dancer perceptions and adjustments and subsequent career commitment contingencies. Her work atmosphere is relatively cooperative, characterized by enduring and friendly interactions with other participants.

The club organization requires her to maintain regular interaction with other members of the establishment. She is responsible for maintaining the prosperity and the cooperative atmosphere. In adjusting to the context of the social club, Nadia has developed friendships and networks of mutual obligation. Because she regards her working environment positively, she wants to continue participating. She likes her coworkers, customers, and management and perceives her work and working environment as enjoyable.

Why does her career persist? Nadia's responses, and those of many of the dancers working at social clubs, indicate that, although participation is no longer essential, continuation is encouraged through the development of personal and moral commitments. That is, not only do dancers feel positively about the people with whom they participate in this activity, but they also feel morally obligated to them and to the establishment in general.

These statements represent dancers' perceptions that the social environment of the social club discourages conflict and hostility, as well as promotes the initiation of positive relations. In addition, it illustrates how dancers feel a sense of responsibility for maintaining the positive atmosphere of the club.

The dancer enforcement of informal rules regarding work attitudes and training of new dancers creates an atmosphere in which dancers have a sense of responsibility for the club. That is, they have invested in the social organization of the club. Continued participation is then essential in order to maintain the social organization they have acted to create. Thus, "successful" dancers in social clubs are those who cooperate with management and fellow dancers, who are sociable, and who can effectively "join" and remain in the established social network.

Consequently, the development of long-term associations promotes the development of moral commitment. That is, dancers develop social ties that encourage them to continue dancing in order to maintain these networks of association. Being successful in the social club environment requires dancers to form friendships; these friendships allow dancers to develop a mutual sense of obligation that dissuades career termination.

Amanda, who reports being in a long-term romantic relationship with a bouncer at her club, demonstrates the strength of these networks: "My friend Nikki [another dancer] got me into dancing. I went to clubs with her. I hang out after work with Gabby and Tara [other dancers], get high with Phil [a customer]." These analyses suggest the social networks that characterize social clubs are influential in both recruiting and maintaining members into exotic dance careers. Most women reported that interest in exotic dance occurred through contact with another woman who was already dancing. This friend was influential in encouraging them to dance as well as providing suggestions and advice. This recruitment practice fosters both personal and moral commitment in that dancers both feel positively about and feel a corresponding sense of moral obligation to their fellow dancers.

6

THE SOCIAL WORLDS
OF EXOTIC DANCE

Going to a strip club is entering a social world, and some social worlds are clearly more empowering/degrading than others. Understandings of why women work in exotic dance must incorporate such constructs as internal and external forces, as well as the larger social circumstances that produce variations in these constructs. Club contexts create working conditions under which various forms of constraint or agency emerge. That is, although there were significant differences across women with regard to how they experience work, this variation appears to be related to the locations in which these women performed their work. What it means to be a dancer as an individual varied across dancers in accordance with cultural definitions and norms as to what it means to be a dancer generically in a particular club. So, given the diversity of these social worlds, why do women in each of these particular social worlds work there?

Just as the experience of dancing differs across clubs, so do the reasons for why they work. Talking with women about their work and why they continued to work in a particular club, I consistently found reasons for working patterned by club typology. In other words, why they danced was conditioned by the worlds in which they danced.

Unpacking explanations of why they danced, I discovered that dancer perception can be generally classified as three phenomenological experiences—individual choice, a sense of connection and

obligation to others, and lack of choice. More specifically, analyses revealed responses that display the three following themes:
dancers *wanted* to dance, *ought* to dance, and/or felt they *had* to
dance. And these perceptions were systematically related to the
type of club (according to the typology) in which they worked.
These findings suggest that each social world's structural features
generate differences in the work and normative order of dancing.
Each of these work and normative orders allow, discourage, or
limit opportunities to form particular relationships with and attitudes toward work, coworkers, clients, and management, which,
in turn, generate distinct phenomenological experiences of work.

In interactions with other members of a social world of exotic
dance, women are exposed to and acquire the norms, values, and
attitudes associated with this career. Involvement in a social world
of exotic dance, like other types of deviant behavior and social
phenomena more generally, involves processes in which dancers
learn how to both do and think about their work. Thus, social
worlds of clubs represent differential social organizations. These
differential social organizations, in turn, present differential experiences of agency and/or constraint. Within each social world, differential association and socialization into varying cultures of
exotic dance and subsequent development of continuity contingencies take place.

Do women feel compelled to dance, are they free agents, or do
they experience both freedom and control in their jobs? In order
to make sense of how these women perform their work with
regard to agency and constraint, I draw on the three-fold commitment framework developed by Johnson (1973, 1991, 1999) and
applied to deviant careers by Ulmer (1994). Michael Johnson, in
his work on commitment, defines three experiences of commitment. Personal commitment is characterized as *wanting to continue*. Moral commitment is characterized as the experience of
feeling as though one *ought to continue*, whether s/he would want
to or not. Finally, structural commitment is described as the experience of feeling as though one is compelled to continue; one feels
as though she *has to continue*, whether she would like to or not.
This work suggests that each commitment stems from different
sources and that one may experience each of these commitments
individually or in combination.

The commitment framework distinguishes personal commitment as an internal choice. Continuity is explained by the individ-

ual personal desires or tastes. Sources for personal commitment include the attitudes toward the line of action, the attitudes toward others with whom one engages in the line of action, and definitions of the self in terms of identities associated with the line of action. Moral commitment is characterized as an internal constraint, created by a sense of moral obligation to others with whom one participates in a line of action, action-specific norms that discourage terminating a particular line of action, and internalized norms regarding consistency in lines of action. Structural commitment is conceptualized as an external constraint. Some sources of structural commitment include the availability/attractiveness of alternatives, the irretrievable investments made, the difficulty of termination, and the social reactions to termination.

My own experience and my observations and interviews suggest that dancers do indeed feel both internal and external agency and constraint. Yes, there are times that dancers feel as though they have to dance. However, at particular times and places, some dancers want to dance. And, interestingly, I found times and places when dancers, including myself, felt an obligation to continue working.

Follow-up interviews and observational data both substantiate dancer descriptions of clubs and suggest that these differences in formal and informal structure were maintained as new dancers became socialized into clubs. These cultural distinctions appeared relatively stable notwithstanding any individual dancer variation. That is, what it means to be a dancer varied across clubs, and these variations perpetuated such that different types of dancer adjustment and commitment patterns consistently developed across clubs.

In the following tables, I provide an organizational framework to clarify my conceptualization of the relationships among club organizational features, dancer perceptions, and subsequent perceptions of dancing. Here I unpack the conceptualization of exotic dance establishments as social worlds, looking specifically at how variations among structural contexts influence subjective experiences and subsequent processual differences in exotic dance career continuity. Specifically, in the following pages I describe the work orders associated with each club type, detailing the practical, logistic organization of work. I show how these conditions produce distinct normative orders—that is, the formal and informal norms and practices. I then outline differences in the resultant sentiment/feeling orders associated with these work and normative orders. In doing so, this book summarizes interclub variation with regard to dancer perceptions of their work and their work contingencies.

Each table represents the variation associated with each phase in the progression of deviant career development. Table 6.1 outlines some of the structural characteristics of clubs; these variations in work order are the foundation of each of the social worlds of exotic dance. While not an exhaustive list, it does present some key differences as to how establishments are organized. Shared combinations of these identified characteristics, such as primary method of money making, customer and dancer population characteristics, club policies, and so on, structure the work of dancing. Thus, these orders are the groundwork that gives rise to particular normative and sentiment orders in which dancers accomplish their goals.

In Table 6.2, I outline the variation in normative orders of clubs. Specifically, I describe variations in the cultural arrangements regarding the practice of work. The previously outlined structural conditions bring about different approaches to informal and formal norms regarding how work is done. Across each work order, I identify distinct patterns as to which aspects of exotic dance are emphasized or deemphasized, as well as how exotic dancers are subculturally portrayed. Across each conglomeration of structural arrangements, there are different work expectations, distinct definitions of dancing, and subsequent unique dancer identities.

As they adjust to their situational circumstances, dancers develop work strategies, attitudes, feelings about their work, and perceptions of the people with whom they work. Table 6.3 describes the particular sentiment order associated with each club typology. It outlines patterns in mind-set, interpersonal interactions, and experience of work across dancers. How dancers think and feel about their work varies substantially, and themes in sentiment can be found across club type.

Work-order features produce varying normative orders and sentiment orders of dancing, which in turn give rise to differences in commitment experiences. Table 6.4 explains variations in dancers' perceptions of career continuity. Specifically, I outline sources of personal, moral, and structural commitment associated

TABLE 6.1
SELECT WORK ORDER FEATURES ACROSS CLUB TYPE

	Hustle Club	Show Club	Social Club
Club Size	Large #customers (50–100) weekdays and weekends	(25-50) Weekdays, (50-100) weekends	Few Customers (<50) weekday and weekend
Number of Dancers	more than 30 dancers/night; high turnover	~10-15 dancers/ night; moderate to limited turnover	~5 dancers/ night; highly stable
Customer Turnover	High level of turnover—few regulars	Few regular customers	Primarily regular customers
Earning Method	Primarily lap dances/champagne rooms	Stage performance/ lap dances	Drinks/stage / informal tipping
Earning Potential	High	High	Low
Typical Customer Demographic	Male-Primarily young; diverse backgrounds; high turnover	Male, young to middle aged; upperclass/ professional high turnover	Male w/ some females, primarily middle aged; working class; stable
Set Characteristics	Few sets; multiple dancers on stage simultaneously; competition for stage time	Approx. 20 minutes; multiple dancers per stage; individual featuring of dancers	Approx. 20 minutes; individual stage time, stage dancing deemphasized in favor of mingling with customers and encouraging them to buy drinks
Booking	N/A	Scheduled by management at management discretion	Negotiated by management & dancer

with each club type. Each club typology induces or discourages particular experiences of commitment by limiting or providing each commitment's respective sources. The club culture, including variations in assumptions, norms, and strategies with regard to the selling of sexual arousal, presents dancers with both opportunities

TABLE 6.2

	Hustle Club	Show Club	Social Club
Alcohol Emphasis	Heavy emphasis on customer consumption; "get them drunk"; liquor limited to champagne rooms to increase sales; dancers sales quotas	Occasional sales quotas; deemphasis on customer alcohol consumption: "drunk patrons are removed"	No sales quotas: regular alcohol consumption among dancers and customers; alcohol sales primary to club
Management Supervision	Minimal, hostile/detached; little monitoring of sexual activity, drug use, conflicts	Extensive; formal monitoring—professional style; limited to auditions, scheduling, and other business-related interactions	Informal, frequent negotiation and interaction; self-regulation among dancers, management involved in social/non-business interactions
Payment	Dancers pay stage fees/tip outs; informally required to make frequent payouts for stage time, dances; high sales requirements—dancers ridiculed/firedif not met; dancers keep percentage of sales	Dancers pay stage fees/tip outs; payments regulated; dancers ridicule selves re: sales; dancers keep percentage of sales	Sales deemphasized; little or no stage fees; dancers may often be paid to work; little attention paid to amount of sales
Dancer Attractiveness Standards	Competitive standards due to high volume of dancers	High standards of attractiveness; strictly enforced	Lenient standards of attractiveness
Atmosphere	Frequent referral to genitalia of dancers/sexual motivations for men; deejay refers to womens' breasts, vaginas, etc.	Frequent referral to dancer performance, beauty; deejay refers to dancers as ladies, sexy, seductive	Frequent referral to dancers by name only; deejays refer to friendly atmosphere, encourages applause
Dancer Identity Expectations	Sex-focused; dancers as objects for sexual gratification	Show focused; dancers as performers	Social-focused; dancers as "girls next door"; barmates

and limitations with regard to the development of commitment. For example, the establishments classified as social clubs are characterized by stable populations with regular collegial interactions. Thus, dancers in these clubs are more likely to experience moral commitment to continuation in exotic dance because the club presents more opportunity to establish the friendship ties and networks of mutual obligation from which moral commitment develops.

These tables outline each layer of analysis. Specifically, I describe the structural characteristics of clubs and then outline the patterns work and normative order associated with each mesomicro dynamics-involved deviant career. That is, work orders are structural precursors of various sources of commitment, operating through the development of particular normative and sentiment orders. Collectively, these tables illustrate the process of exotic dance career development. As they enter the profession, dancers become involved in differential social organizations (each with particular contextual opportunities and constraint) and adjust to accommodate this existing social order. These adjustments, in turn, encourage or discourage the development of particular kinds of commitment. These tables suggest that, although all strip clubs sell sexual arousal, there is substantial variation with regard to accomplishing this task. Variation in such features as management style, customer and dancer composition and turnover, method of money making, and formal and informal norms produce contextual differences in the perceptions and appropriate corresponding behavior associated with the definition of a dancer and the meaning of dancing. That is, organizational variation in the selling of sexual arousal creates differences in club culture. These cultural variations condition the formation of commitments by presenting or limiting different commitment sources.

Throughout my interviews, I tried to capture the phenomenological experience of being a dancer in that particular type of social world. As in most systematic data collection, I asked several of the exact same questions of each of the dancers. Looking at the typical answers to some of these questions across club dancer type reveals substantial differences in the meaning and experience of dancing across social organization. In the following paragraphs, I compare typical ("anchor") responses of dancers across club type as they give brief descriptions of their work environment.

TABLE 6.3
Club Types and Sentiment Orders:
Dancer Interpersonal Relations, Attitudes, and Experiences

	Hustle Club	Show Club	Social Club
Dancer Perceptions of Atmosphere	"This place is a meat market. We're just T&A"; sex-oriented	"We're like goddesses"; display/show oriented, pageant-like atmosphere	"Just like hanging out at a bar with the girl next door"; social oriented
Dancer Attitudes toward Customers	Generally negative: "assholes" and "suckers"	Indifferent	Generally positive, sympathetic: "They're just lonely," "They're usually pretty respectful," "They're just a bunch of good 'ole boys trying to relax after work"
Dancer Attitudes toward Other Dancers	Negative: "bitches"	Indifferent or negative	Friendship cliques/ generally positive
Interaction between Dancers	Competitive/ hostile	Competitive/ detached	Cooperative, friendship networks, much peer regulation, peer initiation processes

THE WORK AND NORMATIVE ORDER
OF THE HUSTLE CLUB

When asked what it was like working at a hustle club, the following quotes were typical responses:

I hate it so much. We're just T and A. It's like a meat market. (Toni, twenty-four, danced six years)

It's like a big assembly line. Each of us comes out, goes to the end, and the others move down. We spend the whole time squatting with our legs spread open. Eventually I think the guys get bored too. There's only so much pussy

TABLE 6.4
DANCER COMMITMENT CONTINGENCIES ACROSS CLUB TYPE

	Hustle Club	Show Club	Social Club
Structural	Prominent; stems from lack of available attractive alternative	Based on irretrievable investments— time, money, effort, training	Less significant than other two types; some social pressure from coworkers
Personal	Weak; stems primarily from potential high earnings for some dancers	Prominent; flows from attachment to show club dancer identity; positive attitude toward dancing (based on emotional and material rewards)	Strong ties to other dancers, positive attitudes toward customers, positive attitude toward club atmosphere/ sociability
Moral	None observed	No significant amount observed	Prominent; significant perceived obligations among dancers, to select customers, management; collective responsibility for club

you can look at 'til they all look the same. (Tia, twenty-four, danced two years)

I hate this place. The girls are bitches here. I've seen girls pissing in each other's bags, stealing . . . One girl put her cigarette out in a new girl's costume bag. These chicks are all skanks and dirty bitches . . . I have to stay here for as long as I can take it. (Connie, twenty-one, danced two years)

The similarity of these quotes illustrates how the negative perceptions of work are systematically related to club structural characteristics. The social world of the hustle club features a detached management style, high levels of turnover, and an emphasis on physical sexual gratification. This context produces a culture in which women experience little agency and personal satisfaction in their work. When the cultural context creates the perception that individuals are expendable, and coworkers are competition, dancers have little opportunity or motivation to engage in the genuine enduring interactions through which the favorable attitudes toward a line or action and feelings of mutual obligation that underlie personal and moral commitment develop. Rather, dancers become disassociated with their labor and view their work, as well as others with whom they participate in this course of action, negatively.

Explaining Career Continuity: The World of the Hustle Club

Given the hostile, competitive, degrading conditions of work, one wonders why anyone would work in such an establishment. Structural commitments are experienced as external constraints on desistance from exotic dancing. In other words, dancers may maintain their employment in hustle clubs when they develop structural commitments that compel to them to do so. One common source of structural commitment is the perception among hustle club dancers that they do not have attractive alternatives to dancing available to them.

> M: Why do you work here?
> Why am I here? 'Cuz, shit, I can't do anything else. I'm not good at that nine to five stuff, and I can't pass no drug test. So it sucks here, but it's better than nothing. I got two kids and rent and shit. (Skylar, twenty-eight, danced five years)

Consistent with Johnson's ideas, my interviews with women working in the social world of the hustle club indicated that they were structurally committed to dancing. That is, they felt as though they had little choice. Not surprisingly, many of these women found little personal satisfaction from dancing. Structural commitments compelled them to continue exotic dancing. In other words, dancers maintained their employment in hustle clubs because they developed structural obstacles to quitting; external pressures kept them from quitting, regardless of any potential internal motivation to do so. One common source of structural commitment was the perception among hustle club dancers that they did not have attractive alternatives to dancing available to them.

Although the level of success may depend on other factors (such as physical appearance or personality characteristics), employment in exotic dance has no educational or skill requirement. Dancers may lack the skills or education to obtain more conventional employment. Also, participation in exotic dancing does not qualify an individual for other employment. Indeed, identifying oneself as an exotic dancer may limit potential job opportunities due to the stigma associated with its deviant label.

Furthermore, conventional employment may not be perceived as suitable for their lifestyle. Dancing may rank higher in job qualities than the other occupations perceived to be available to them. That is, they may perceive dancing to be the quickest and most efficient way to meet their financial and childcare needs.

Brianna's story illustrates how the dancer perceptions, adjustment, and subsequent commitment contingencies are influenced by the social organization of the hustle club world. Her work atmosphere was competitive and sexually emphasized, characterized by management apathy and dancer disposability. Brianna's customers saw her only as an object for their sexual gratification.

In the world of the hustle club, dancers, like Brianna, must continually struggle to maintain their physical boundaries and deal with sexual coercion. Not only did management not respond to her needs, but management practices exacerbated her situation. She was not cared about; she was simply an anonymous dancer, just like all the others. She could not complain; she had to tolerate their unfair working conditions and management policies. Her coworkers also intensified her feeling of hostility and frustration; they were threats to the livelihood that she struggled to earn.

In response to these circumstances, Brianna became aggressive to her fellow dancers. She lacked the power to confront her employer (she would lose her job) and her customers (they were essential for money making). However, because all dancers shared essentially equivalent relative power, she could channel her frustrations and resentment into her interactions with fellow colleagues.

For her, dancing, although clearly an unsatisfying occupation, was better than her low-skilled and corresponding low-paying employment alternatives. Perceiving that there were no attractive alternatives available to her, she felt externally constrained to continue dancing. Her participation was limited to include only times of economic need. Rather than choosing freely to work as a dancer, she danced only when she perceived that this involvement was necessary due to the financial need and limited options that constrained her.

Why did her career persist? Brianna's responses indicate that although she experienced little fulfillment with her job and no ties to the people with whom she shared her social world, she will most likely continue her involvement in this profession. The social conditions of the hustle club do not provide opportunities for the development of friendship ties or personal identification with a profession that might otherwise encourage someone to remain involved in a specific behavior or social world.

Rather, Brianna's experience, and that of many of the dancers working at hustle clubs, was one of structural constraint. She perceived her situation in terms of the structural conditions that compelled her to continue. That is, she had little education and no other marketable job skills. Her compulsion to continue originated from her perception of her available options, which included waiting tables, tending bar, or "flipping burgers," as less attractive than her current occupation.

Although she disavowed her involvement, claiming that she "quit a hundred times," her description reveals a cycle of perpetual financial need, fulfilled by dancing. Under these circumstances, there is a high likelihood that there would continue to be moments of perceived financial necessity and subsequent involvement in dancing to meet these needs. Thus, what began as an easy way to make "some quick cash" developed into structural commitments that promoted future continued participation in dancing.

Dancers at hustle clubs most often described their occupation using negative terminology; such descriptions included the terms *stressful, degrading, horrible, demeaning, "sucks," frustrating, hell, awful,* and *abusive.* Furthermore, it became apparent that participation in exotic dance at such establishments only perpetuates the cycle of declining attractive alternatives.

That is, these women work at the clubs because they feel they have no choice; yet their participation precludes them from taking the actions necessary to present better alternatives later. Thus, in these establishments, it appears that the longer a woman danced, the more structural constraints she reported experiencing. Consistent with a process Becker (1960) called "unfitting," women reported that their previous choices and adjustment to their present situation or roles restricts the availability/attractiveness of future alternatives.

> I'm thirty years old and have no education. I wanted to go to college when I was younger, but I never got around to it. Dancing was fun and easy cash, and I have a son to raise. What the hell am I supposed to do now? I'm miserable, but who's gonna give a woman with no education and no skills a job? So, I'll just keep dancing for as long as I can. (Andrea, twenty-nine, danced eleven years)

This quote illustrates the development of structural commitment to exotic dancing. For these dancers, early involvement in dancing limits later opportunities. Although participation may have initially involved internal choice, being a dancer has since made them "unfitting" for other employment. Consequently, although they no longer feel personal satisfaction with their jobs, they feel that they have no choice. Thus, they are structurally committed to dancing in that they perceive that their actions are constrained and continued participation is compulsory.

Although the majority of hustle clubs were located in large cities, I did observe a club with similar social organizational features in a rural area. Although smaller in scale with regard to number of dancers and size of customer population, dancer turnover remained high. Dancers frequently reported working there very rarely, preferring to pursue other avenues of money making and rely on dancing there only in times of dire financial need. One dancer referred to the club as her "last stop. It's a last resort."

This establishment exhibited a similar lack of policy enforcement regarding drug and alcohol use and physical touching of dancers. Like in other hustle clubs, in this club dancers spent little time on stage or in the dressing room, most often "working the floor," walking around selling dances to customers.

The regular practice of having dancers fraternize with customers in an unsupervised atmosphere presented an opportunity for open, unwanted sexual contact. Furthermore, this practice and lack of management interest in enforcing no-touching policies resulted in negative characterizations of what it means to be a dancer in this establishment. Dancers' subsequent perceptions of and situational adjustments to the club context were characteristically similar to those found among other hustle club establishments.

Women frequently reported being touched or grabbed. I observed several patrons reaching under dancers' tops or skirts while women attempted to persuade them to buy dances. Other customers considered this behavior nonoffensive; many regarded it as humorous. Management did not respond in any way to this behavior. The lack of response to such behavior perpetuated a permissive atmosphere toward the degrading and sexual harassment of women. Management apathy discouraged dancers from responding negatively. Rather, dancers were persuaded to tolerate or even encourage this behavior in order to facilitate "hustling" and making the owner some money.

The pressure to sell dances and the nonenforcement of touching policies acted so that dancers were limited in their ability to respond to physical advances. Dancers most often concealed their contempt or aversion, often pretending to be mildly amused or treating the men like naughty children. Typical responses were, "Now, now. If you wanna do that, you gotta buy a dance," or, "Be good." Interviews with dancers indicate that although they frequently reported feeling violated, angry, or even disgusted, they perceived that they must tolerate being touched in order to make sales. Women were encouraged by management to do whatever necessary to sell lap dances; dancers made roughly forty percent of the profit from these sales.

As one dancer stated: "There are no rules, except no prostitution. I think they'd even allow that if they weren't scared of getting busted. I know it's going on around here, but we pretend it's not allowed. Everything else is allowed. And some guys get pretty grabby back there. Guys are always fuckin' touching you or trying to lick your pussy and shit . . . most of the time, they want you to grind them off [rub her pelvis against them to elicit ejaculation] . . . Dances cost twenty-five dollars, but Tommy [the owner] takes fifteen of it. So I'm only making ten bucks, while this dude's trying to put his tongue up my [vagina]" (Roxanna, twenty-two, danced two years).

Dancers at this establishment discussed comparable adjustments to their environment. Like other hustle club dancers, all indicated that they felt frustrated and powerless. Many women perceived management as corrupt and defined their situations as exploitative. Dancers stated that getting high or drunk was essential in order to perform their jobs; most reported regular use of marijuana, heroine, and/or cocaine. Yet, when questioned, most admitted that dancing was necessary to fund continued drug use as well. Lacking personal satisfaction or identity with their jobs or other dancers, women regarded their careers as an experience of structural commitment. That is, they felt trapped into continuing to dance due to their relative lack of financial alternatives.

This finding suggests that this club typology is not limited to urban areas. Rather, the atmosphere of the club, individual adjustment and negotiation strategies to the atmosphere, and subsequent commitment developments are not geographically bound. Rather, they are a product of the discrete social organizational features of the club, including management style, policies, and method of money making.

THE WORK AND NORMATIVE ORDER OF THE SHOW CLUB

When asked what it was like working at a show club, the following quotes were typical responses.

> You've gotta bust your ass to keep yourself up [maintain physical attractiveness]. You can't get fat. And you can do that [stay thin] a couple of ways. One is by working out; the other is lipo. I can't work out. It's too hard. I used to try that, and it did nothing for me. So now I just get lipo—just suck it out. It costs about two thousand dollars or so, but then the fat's gone. I've already had it twice, once around my stomach and lower back, and once around my hips and ass. But I'm starting to gain some back. So I'll probably have to do it again. (Layla, thirty-one, danced twelve years)

> When I'm on stage, it's rush. The minute I step on the stage, I'm in the zone, and the dancer in me takes over. And I'm a great dancer. Some of these women can't do shit. But I can dance. (Shanna, twenty-eight, danced ten years)

The social world of the show club features a detached management style, a restrictive selection criteria, and an emphasis on performance. This social organization creates a culture in which
dancing is individually focused. Power becomes defined less in
terms of management relations and control over working conditions and more in terms of internal drive to attain the goal of
"ideal." Thus, this environment produces a "culture of perfection."

Explaining Career Continuity: The World of the Show Club

Why do dancers participate in the social world of the show club?
Why would they participate in an environment in which they are
required to continually meet such high standards of beauty? One
potential explanation behind career continuity is the development
of structural commitment. Once employed in show clubs, dancers
spend time, money, and effort to acquire the techniques, skills, and
materials necessary for success. Dancers may regard these expenditures as *irretrievable investments*. That is, dancers have exerted
an enormous amount of time, energy, and effort to become or
maintain the "ideal" fantasy. These dancers may then feel that
continued participation in exotic dance *is necessary in order to
reap returns on these expenses*.

When asked why they would work at a show club, dancers
gave the following responses:

> I get told how gorgeous I am all night. There's nothing
> wrong with that. And yeah, they have to pay me. They
> have to pay me for my attention. They work hard all
> week to make money and then hand it all over to me on a
> Saturday night. It's not demeaning to me; it's demeaning
> to them. They give me money 'cuz that's all they have to
> give. (Erica, twenty-five, danced three years)

> I absolutely love dancing on stage. With the pole and the
> lights, it's much more like entertaining . . . It's almost the-
> atrical. (Stasha, twenty-two, danced four months)

> I can be with my boyfriend and hear him bitch. Mean-
> while, I come to work and everyone tells me how beauti-
> ful I am. (Amanda, twenty-one, danced three years)

Another subject describes her "need" to dance as her opportunity to engage in the role performance associated with show club dancing: "I feel like I can be someone different. Jess [her real name] is boring, but Gem can be a royal bitch. Sometimes I have to dance to get it out" (Gem, danced four years).

Because of the individualistic character associated with their work, the detached management style, and the restricted nature of client-dancer interaction, dancers in this environment do not have the opportunity to develop social networks with their coworkers, management, or clients. They are limited in their ability to pursue genuine, enduring interactions. Subsequently, dancers do not explain their career persistence in terms of moral commitment, as they experience relatively little sense of obligation to the other with which they participate in this course of action.

Instead, dancers at show clubs frequently indicated that they desired attention and admiration, specifically for their beauty. Many reported participating in other current or aspiring occupations that focus on physical attractiveness, such as modeling, bikini contests, or working as waitresses at adult-themed restaurants (e.g., Hooters). Respondents indicated that the show club environment was the best or only atmosphere in which they received this highest level of validation of their physical beauty. For these women, continuation in exotic dance provided them with the satisfaction and validation they could not receive elsewhere.

This means that in addition to the structural conditions that compel women to continue dancing, they may also perceive persistence in dancing as an internal choice. That is, Rachel's experience, and that of many of the dancers working in show clubs, was one of both structural and personal commitment. She defined herself in terms of an identity mobilized by her participation in the show club. For her, dancing was her identity. The clubs had strict standards; she made substantial investment in order to successfully meet these requirements. In return, she perceived meeting these expectations as a source of satisfaction and viewed her success in this environment as a source of her identity.

Moreover, show club dancers have a great deal of difficulty in terminating their careers because of the intense personal satisfaction associated with being a "good performer." These dancers often described dancing in terms of a "rush" or "thrill." Dancers who had transitioned out of dancing often described a state of anxiety that arose when visiting an exotic dance establishment.

These women stated that, when driving by or patronizing an exotic dance establishment, they missed dancing immensely. When these women heard about a particularly busy night from other dancers still involved in dancing, they yearned to have been there and participated in the events of that evening. These "validation returns" and "performance highs" are sources of personal commitment that are unique to show clubs. One dancer described her experience: "If it's packed and the crowd's really goin', I just start thinking' about it—how I should get up there and wow them. I get so jealous. It just kills me to not dance on a night like that" (Kia, twenty-seven, danced six years).

Similarly, Claire, a former show club dancer for more than 5 years, stated: "I really miss it sometimes. I miss the stage. There's something to it. I was really good at it. I see these girls up here, and I think, make it last as long as you can . . . If I could go back, I'd have started sooner. Heck, I still wanna get up there and strut my stuff, especially on a big night."

Just as winning a pageant requires investment and can be a source of pride, and the corresponding title of "beauty queen" can become incorporated into an individual's identity, being a good performer becomes integral to the show club dancer's sense of self and consequently motivates her to continue dancing. Hence, in addition to necessitating the making of investments that *require* her to continue in order to obtain compensation, the social conditions rewarded Rachel so as to make her to *want* to continue.

Interviews with other show club dancers corroborate Rachel's experiences and subsequent definition of self in terms of the "dancer" identity: "I had a regular [customer] once tell me that any guy who tries to get me to stop hasn't seen me at work . . . or he would know that it's me. That's my thing. And I believe that" (Ivy, twenty-seven, danced seven years).

Dancers at show clubs consistently indicated that being successful in exotic dancing involved considerable irrevocable investments. Investments undertaken by dancers deemed essential for success in show clubs frequently have little value elsewhere. For example, the effort required to learn "pole work," cannot easily pay off in other occupations. Other investment efforts, although they may potentially reap rewards in conventional society, are most directly rewarded through continuation in exotic dance. For example, although undergoing breast augmentation might be seen by women who are not involved in dancing as beneficial in some ways, breast enlargement is most directly rewarded by continued participation in exotic dancing. In other words, career persistence is essential in order for a dancer who has undergone this procedure to reap "returns."

As well as enduring physical pain and the costs associated with cosmetic enhancement, most women in show clubs reported spending a large amount of time and effort to develop and practice routines; the efforts encourage them to continue working. Such time and effort expenditures are additional sources of *structural commitment* to continue in the course of action of exotic dancing in that dancers feel *continued participation is required in order to receive the benefits of their expended efforts.* For example, most dancers must develop their dance and pole-work skills in order to successfully compete at show clubs. However, this expertise does not easily transfer into most conventional occupations. Continued participation in exotic dancing may then be the only avenue available for dancers to display and be rewarded for these abilities. In order to reap the benefits of these investments, dancers feel compelled to continue dancing.

In addition to the financial return on investments, dancers at show clubs were also seeking validation returns. Show club dancing is highly profitable. Yet, for many of the show club dancers, dancing is perceived less in terms of attractive financial alternatives and more in terms of validation and personal rewards. To be successful at this occupation, show club dancers must strive to become the ideal image of a client's fantasy. Once dancers have accomplished this goal, they then seek affirmation of their success. One dancer discusses her experience: "I like being a goddess. I've worked really hard to look good; it doesn't come cheap. I definitely wanna hear about it" (Kia, twenty-seven, danced six years).

This statement demonstrates that, in addition to the financial benefit, show club dancers may be *personally motivated* to continue dancing by their need for admiration. In other words, "being picked" is intrinsically rewarding; it acts to validate that their efforts are not in vain; they have achieved the goal of being their most alluring. Just as not being selected is viewed as an individual failure, being selected is perceived as a validation of their beauty.

Moreover, the ability to make the structural commitments to dance is often framed as a source of personal commitment. Involvement in show dancing requires substantial investments. Although these investments structurally encourage continuation, career persistence among these dancers is primarily experienced as personal commitment. Not all women are willing or able to spend the time, money, and effort necessary to be successful show club dancers. Thus, those women who do take pride in their determination and sacrifice are able to achieve a goal that other women cannot. In other words, being able to make the investments necessary and meet these expectations becomes personally satisfying, and validation of this success becomes a critical element of dancers' definitions of self.

Women also regarded their work as personally enjoyable. Many show club dancers reported that they danced in order to feel good about themselves. For these women, dancing provided an atmosphere where they were openly praised or admired. They were motivated to continue dancing in order to continue to receive this praise.

One example of the personal enjoyment of show dancing involves the construction of an "ideal" self. Show club dancers often talk of "getting into character," indicating how dancers frequently view show club performances as an opportunity to assume a different identity. Many stated that while performing, they "could be whatever they chose"; most often this entailed being uninhibited or exhibitionistic. Women reported that show club dancing was the only place where they "could be that type of person."

In this way, exotic dancing at a show club is characteristically similar to other types of performance, such as acting, modeling, and other dancing. Consequently, consistent with many of the current studies written by exotic dancers that express satisfaction and professional pride in exotic dancing, show club dancers often described dancing in terms of performance. Exotic dancers in show clubs demonstrated a great deal of physical skill and attractiveness, athleticism, and other performance abilities. Many dancers stated that they had tried to terminate their careers previously but found other occupations less fulfilling. Being successful at this occupation, giving a good performance, can be a source of confidence, enjoyment, and satisfaction.

In addition to physical adjustments required while working in a show club, individual dancers must engage in a negotiation between ideal and actual selves. This involves a role performance in which they must alter their personalities so as to entice their audience. In addition to cultivating their beauty and dance abilities, dancers must manipulate their behavior and attitudes so as to convey emotions to potential customers. Some emotions that dancers must convey include appearing aroused, excited, happy, friendly, outgoing, seductive, innocent, confident, shy, sleazy, or aggressive.

While many women reported occasional difficulty in manipulating their emotions, or "getting psyched," show club dancers often regarded this manipulation positively. Dancers often said that the role performance involved in show club dancing offered them the opportunity to express an "alter ego": "I love being Autumn. I get to cut loose and shit. Sometimes I can't turn it off and still feel crazy when I get home. My husband says he loves Karri [her real name], but Autumn is a great fuck" (Autumn, thirty-seven, danced ten years). "I've always wanted to be a dancer—not necessarily a stripper. But there was always some part of me that wanted to walk around and pose. I remember being six, finding my dad's *Playboy*, and copying all the poses" (Vega, twenty-seven, danced nine years).

The provision of "validation returns" consistent with show clubs not only foster personal commitment; it also acts so that dancers become, to some extent, structurally committed to dancing. They strive for admiration and perceive exotic dancing as the best way to obtain it. Many often indicated that their romantic partners did not provide a sufficient amount of praise or affection. Dancing, therefore, became an attractive alternative to meet this perceived deficiency. "I told my old man that he should come see me at work. I want him to see me up there . . . [M]aybe he'd realize just how good he has it . . . that on any night there are plenty of guys who'd beg to be with me" (Angela, twenty-seven, danced five years). "My exboyfriend came to see me once, while we were together. He got all jealous. He freaked out. I think it got to him to see all these guys wanting me. He'd never really seen me like that before . . . I loved it. It was like, 'See how lucky you are, buddy?'" (Kia, twenty-seven).

These experiences parallel Hochschild's (1979) discussion of the changing dynamics of home and work in modern American society. Specifically, Hochschild finds that often men and women "fled the pressures of home" for the relief of work. These individuals reported that home life is often stressful, that children, spouses, and housework are frequently demanding, and that domestic relationships are perpetually unsatisfying. These individuals regarded their work environment as preferable to these negative conditions.

Similarly, dancers in show clubs often indicated that their intimate relationships were unsatisfying. This dissatisfaction was primarily associated with their husbands, boyfriends, or other dating partners. Many dancers stated that their romantic partners often failed to maintain stable and gainful employment, had drug or alcohol problems, or were neglectful; relationships between dancers and their romantic partners were often hostile, adulterous, quarrelsome, or disaffected. Many dancers described their romantic partners "assholes," "losers," "drunks," or "bums."

In contrast, the conditions of the show club create an atmosphere in which dancers are surrounded by a group of attentive admirers. In response to the negative feeling associated with their partners, many dancers prefer being at work because their "real" relationships are unfulfilling and fail to meet both their financial and their emotional needs.

Furthermore, the organizational features of show club dancing that make it an attractive alternative also cultivate personal commitment development. That is, the glamour, attention, and status that women perceive as best attained through show club dancing act as potential personal rewards that encourage further participation. Although preexisting structural circumstances may require dancers to make substantial investments, the perceived return on these investments goes beyond simply financial return to include personal satisfaction.

Continued participation in dancing is fostered not only by the investments of time, money, and energy required to get there but also by the satisfaction associated with having made these investments and being rewarded. Thus, the ability to push one's self to achieve the highest standards of beauty and ability becomes satisfying. To this extent, the investment of resources becomes intrinsically rewarding, commitment to dancing is perpetuated through these personal commitment mechanisms.

Why did Rachel continue to dance? Rachel's responses, and those of many of the dancers working at show clubs, indicate that, although participation is no longer essential, continuation is encouraged through the development of structural and personal commitment. That is, dancers feel they must continue to participate in this activity in order to reap the rewards of the investments they have incurred. In addition, being able to meet these high expectations becomes a source of satisfaction and self-esteem. In other words, when "being picked" is defined as the goal of this environment, and individuals have invested a substantial amount of effort in order to be picked, meeting that goal and being picked become sources of pleasure and identity.

Rachel's narrative illustrates how dancer perceptions and negotiation strategies are influenced by the social organization of the show club. Her work atmosphere was performance and beauty oriented. To be successful at this type of club requires a dancer to be her most glamourous and beautiful. In response to these contextual conditions, Rachel then adjusted her behavior to achieve and maintain the expectations of her environment. Her success in the show club subsequently became a source of professional pride and a validation of her beauty. That is, this environment provided her the opportunity to develop personal commitment in that being a "successful" dancer became both *satisfying* and a source of *personal identity.*

By and large, the organizational structure, policies, and norms of the show club world create structural and personal commitment contingencies that encourage exotic dance career persistence. The validation process and pageantlike atmosphere of the show club provide an opportunity for admiration, excitement, and positive feelings about one's appearance; in other words, unlike other establishments, the social world of the show club, while requiring substantial investments in order to participate, gives dancers the opportunity for the glamour that is otherwise unattainable in their everyday lives. The glamour associated with show clubs fosters structural and personal commitment development as it acts as both a reward on dancer investments and a significant source of personal validation and self-worth.

The social organizational features of the show club, including highly restrictive selection criteria, detached management style, "showcasing" of performers, and an emphasis professional performance produces a culture that encourages self-improvement. Thus, adjustment to this working environment requires dancers to continually invest in the development and maintenance of their abilities and appearance. This investment acts to structurally obligate women to continue dancing in that they *must* continue dancing in order to reap the benefits of these investments. In addition, the validation practices characteristic of show clubs lead dancers to *want* to continue; find their jobs personally satisfying and a source of self-image Thus, being a dancer in a show club becomes connected to a dancer's identity, and subsequently encourages a dancer to continue her participation.

In *The Fence* (1986), Steffensmeier describes the initiation, persistence, and desistence contingencies involved in the career of "Sam Goodman," a professional fence. He notes that one obstacle Sam faces in terminating his career in the buying and selling of stolen goods is the thrill or excitement that accompanies a "good score." Thus, even when Sam has a profitable legitimate business, no longer needs to engage in criminal activity, and faces a substantial personal and professional costs if arrested, he still finds opportunities for good scores enticing. Sam believes that his involvement has endured so long and he has become so skilled that he has "larceny in his heart."

Show club dancers experiences parallel this phenomenon. Many show club dancers cited the "need" to perform as a significant obstacle to terminating exotic dance careers. Indeed, in circumstances in which dancers were no longer financially motivated to work, many women stated that they could not resist dancing when given the opportunity to "really perform." The excitement and sense of satisfaction associated with dancing were often described as a "performance high." Indeed, many women working in show clubs described themselves as "addicted to stripping." "Some nights are your nights. I had nights where I was 'on'—sold all the dances—where everyone was cheering for me. It's like I could do no wrong. I mean it's awesome. The other girls are all wondering, 'what makes *her* so damn special?' It's like a total rush, and I go home like 'I love dancing!'" (Cameron, twenty, danced six months).

Observational data and interviews with many of the women employed in show clubs suggest that participation on any given night can be exhilarating. For Cameron, and many dancers in similar circumstances, a "good night" was perceived less in terms of financial gain. Rather, dancers think about the rewards of their involvement in terms of prevailing over their competitors and the pleasure associated with being admired. Yet this contest occurs every night; consequently, the personal satisfaction that results from being selected on any one particular night is fleeting. Continued participation is then essential to maintain levels of personal satisfaction.

THE WORK AND NORMATIVE ORDER
OF THE SOCIAL CLUB

When asked what it was like working in a social club, the following quotes were typical responses of the dancers:

> Al [the owner] is this old biker dude . . . He's there all the time. He's pretty laid back . . . We usually don't really need him to do much. We handle things ourselves. If a girl's doing somethin' . . . we don't let that go on. We're not mean to her or anything, for all we know she could be really hard up and desperate. But one of us will tell her that we know what she's doin' and that's not cool here . . . Let's just all agree to not do that shit . . . If a guy is being rude to the girls, trying to touch 'em or getting obnoxious, we'll tell . . . Al will kick him out and not let him come back. (Savannah, twenty-six, danced four years)

> No bullshit . . . This place is pretty cool—laid back. You don't make much, but it's a lot of fun. (Haley, twenty-three, danced three years)

Social club environments, with smaller, more stable populations, little competition among dancers, and a deemphasis on sexual gratification offer dancers more symmetrical power relationships and foster networks of mutual obligation among individual dancers, their coworkers, and management. Socialization into this culture entails developing and maintaining dense social networks.

These networks of influence expose women to definitions favorable toward their work and other participants with whom they interact. Dancers feel personally responsible in the recruiting and indoctrinating of fellow dancers; they become individually responsible for maintaining both the culture and the prosperity of the club and each other. Such features are the personal and moral commitment mechanisms by which dancers become differentially associated into the establishment. Career persistence among these dancers is experienced as personal and moral commitment in that dancers continue dancing both out of a personal desire to continue and in order to fulfill their moral obligations to others with whom they participate in this activity.

Explaining Career Continuity: The World of the Social Club

Given the limited income opportunity, why do women work in social clubs? Observations and interviews with social club dancers suggest that structural conditions foster both internal choice and internal constraints that perpetuate exotic dance careers. Most of the women discussed their continued participation in dancing at the social club in terms of personal preference and internal responsibility. Dancing at the social club is less about money and more about meeting and maintaining other relationships, having a good time and developing networks of interaction. Those in smaller, more stable clubs are more likely to maintain existing friendships, develop social networks, and have symmetrical power relationships with management. These factors increase the likelihood that dancers will both enjoy their jobs and develop a sense of loyalty or obligation to the establishment and networks in which they "belong." When asked why they worked at a show club, dancers gave the following answers:

> I always come in here. I've been working here for, like, eight years. I'm in here all the time. We all decided to drop in and see Brenda (bartender). I'm never quitting (sarcastically). Ain't that right, Brenda? (Devon, twenty-six, danced eight years)

> I like most of the people I work with. I have my regular customers, and I enjoy having my regular friends around. (Jasmine, thirty-four, danced twelve years)

> I really don't want to go [to a club to work]. I just wanna stay home. But Jesse [another dancer] is hard up; her bills are overdue, and she doesn't wanna go alone. So I told her I'd go along. (Gem, age, dance career not provided)

> What else would I do on Saturday night? All my friends are here. So even if I go to the bars, I end up stopping in here. (Diva, twenty-six, danced seven years)

For many of these women, being a dancer in this type of club was characterized as very positive. The title of "dancer" was associated with sociability, popularity, and fun. That is, women in social clubs felt closely tied to their identities as dancers as well as the establishments in which they worked. Many indicated that working in these clubs was personally satisfying.

In addition to being a source of personal commitment, the social club recruitment processes and promotion of collegial relations play a critical role in the development of moral commitment. As well as the positive feelings associated with liking the other dancers, the initiation of new dancers encourages the development of moral commitment by appealing to a dancer's sense of loyalty to those who have, in a sense, become her "mentors." Thus, dancers in social clubs feel internally constrained. That is, dancers who become identified as reliable must continue to work in order to remain identified as such. As a consequence, they are then inclined to work when they may otherwise prefer not to and do not have to; rather they "ought to" in order to align their behavior with internalized consistency norms.

The smaller and more stable number of dancers in social clubs creates a dependency between dancers and management. Establishments require at least a certain number of dancers in order to open, so dancers need a certain number of other dancers to show up in order for everyone to make money. In blue-collar towns and areas with more stable populations, clubs have fewer women who are both willing and able to dance. Therefore, club owners are more motivated to attract and keep dancers.

One way of doing this is by being flexible in negotiating booking schedules. In social clubs, bookings [the scheduling of specific dancers to work] are often coordinated between dancer and club needs. Dancers stated that club owners often consider a dancer's specific needs when making bookings. For example, if a dancer needs to work in order to meet a dire financial concern, the owner of a social club may book her on a given night, although the club already has a sufficient number of dancers scheduled. As Andrea, a longtime dancer at a social club, explained: "There are a lot of girls on the schedule tonight—too many. But I'm trying to get a down payment on a house, so I really need to work. I was already scheduled, and then Nadia called Al and asked to get booked as many nights as she could this week. Apparently she's trying to get up some money to pay for her wedding coming up. So Al went ahead and booked her too."

Ava discussed a similar experience: "I'm getting divorced. My ex took everything. He even sold my costumes when I left. So I have nothing. I don't have shit. I'm back living at my mom's. So I called up Al and told him I needed to work. He went ahead and put me on all week."

Three- and six-month follow-up interviews with Ava revealed that she is now currently romantically involved with the owner's son. She now regularly works two to three days per week, as well as whenever Al "needs girls." Her statements illustrate how the mutualism of management and dancer relations induces feelings of obligation: "They [management] put me on [the schedule] when he [Al] hadn't seen me in forever—just 'cuz he knew me and remembered that I was a good girl. So, yeah, sure I'll come in—if they need girls."

The management's willingness to "take in" those needing help is well known among dancers. Upstairs, the club has a number of small, modesty furnished motel rooms, with a shared bathroom. Several dancers reported staying in these rooms, without pay, during brief periods between housing or during times of economic difficulty. Three dancers indicated that they were permitted to reside at the club without charge for a month or longer.

Haley, a Jonston native and longtime dancer at Fantasy, had been occupying one of the rooms for over a month. She stated: "I'm staying here for a little while. Alex and I broke up, and we were living together in [a neighboring town], so I was driving back and forth, but then I had to move back. So Al's letting me stay here for a little while while I get myself together and figure out what I'm gonna do. I just need to take a step back for bit and figure out what I'm doing. I'm thinking about what I wanna do— maybe enrolling in massage school. I gotta do something, and the school has job placement and financial aid. I'm thinking about that and trying to get a place with Leah, but we gotta come up with the deposit."

The "taking in" approach to management is a structural feature distinct to social clubs. Although only a few other social clubs had rooms specifically set aside for dancers, dancers reported that the provision of accommodations, such as spare bedrooms, guaranteed transportation to and from work, and temporary use of vehicles is a common custom. Such practices are conducted formally, such as with posted signs denoting accommodation availability, as well as informally, through the development of carpools and specific requests. For example, a dancer at a social club may call the club that evening to report that her car is in need of repair. In response, the owner or bar manager will either pick her up or call another dancer who is also scheduled to work and ask if she will bring her along.

The unique management style of the social club, which includes a willingness to take into account dancer preferences and the provision of housing, is a significant source of moral commitment. Policies of the social club management evoke norms of reciprocity and a deep sense of loyalty among dancers. That is, as owners make concessions to meet dancers' needs, dancers are then more willing to meet the needs of the club in exchange. Through this reciprocity, dancers develop moral commitments; they feel obligated to work when they otherwise would not so as to ensure the prosperity of the club and the other dancers.

Such perceptions of moral commitment are not limited to dancer relations with club owners but extend to customers as well. Dancers with smaller and more stable customer and dancer populations are necessarily characterized by regular and enduring interactions. Dancers consistently interact with the same customers over and over. As a consequence, they have the opportunity to develop informal social networks that include customers. These networks encourage dancer career persistence by eliciting feelings of obligation. Specifically, dancers may work when they otherwise would not in order to meet the perceived expectations of their regular clients. The following quotes show how dancers in social clubs are motivated to work by their feeling of obligation to customers and perceptions that particular customers are expecting them to be there.

> I don't wanna work all the time. But *the club needs me sometimes* [emphasis added]. They only have three girls tonight. I don't want this place to close. I can dance anywhere, but I like it here. I just wish we'd get some more girls, so I could chill out more. (Sasha, twenty-six, danced four years)

> I wasn't going to come in, but I promised I'd show Tasha some moves. She's new. She needs some help with the pole [learning how to do pole work], so I told her I would help her out. (Mikki, danced five years)

I don't really feel like it [working tonight], but I told
Frank [a regular customer] I'd see him tonight. (Tasha,
twenty, danced one month)

The intense rivalries that frequently exist between establishments provide further evidence of dancers' moral commitment to
clubs. Specifically, dancers often described other establishments
using "us" and "them" terminology, frequently refusing to dance
at other clubs. The rivalry and negative perceptions of other clubs
appear independent of actual knowledge of or experiences in these
clubs. The following description, from a longtime dancer at a
social club, characterizes the development of club cliques: "This is
the only club in town, except for Mermaids. And none of the Fantasy girls wanna work there. That club's run by these two dancers.
They're sisters and complete bitches; they have a clique. They
think they're all that 'cuz they've been there forever, and so they
run the show. They are catty and try to start gossip and crap—like
in high school or somethin'. So usually all the girls that come from
Mermaids try to play that catty gossip . . . So if a girl wants to
work, she's got here or there, and none of us want to go there"
(Sierra, twenty-seven, danced five years).
    Mermaids is also a social club and highly characteristically
consistent with Fantasy. Notably, interviews with dancers from
Mermaids indicated similar opinions regarding the dancers and
management at Fantasy. That is, although observational data indicate that both clubs share much of the same organization features,
dancers at Mermaids regarded "their club" as a preferable environment relative to Fantasy. These perceptions appear to be culturally proscribed beliefs, in that, among both Mermaids and
Fantasy dancers, negative evaluations of the dancers and working
conditions of the other club existed independent of respondents
ever having actually worked there.
    This club rivalry highlights the loyalty dancers feel toward the
clubs where they work and speaks to the internal constraints experienced among dancers at social clubs. In other words, "their club"
becomes a place where they belong; this membership corresponds
to responsibility. This responsibility includes not only socializing
new dancers but also maintaining the success of the club.
    In addition to continuing participation out of feelings of loy-
alty to club management and clients, career persistence is also
encouraged by the popular use of social connections as recruiting

networks among dancers in social clubs. This initiation and "mentoring" process is a feature unique to social establishments. Social club dancers were more likely than dancers in other clubs to have been recruited through preexisting friendships or acquaintanceships. Therefore, social club dancers were more likely to regard their coworkers positively as these preexisting positive feelings were instrumental in the initiation of their careers.

Many of the women employed in social clubs report being involved in a social network of coworkers and customers. In fact, dancers frequently indicated that coworkers and customers are their closest or most frequently contacted friends. They report regularly "hanging out" with other dancers or customers, often even dating or having romantic relationships within this social network.

The organization of the club prevents dancer antagonism and promotes a collective atmosphere. Dancers adjust to this environment by using negotiation strategies of cooperation and friendship formation. Thus, dancers regard fellow dancers as friends rather than competition. These friendships are the foundation for the development of moral commitment to career persistence.

The positive feelings for one's coworkers are a source of personal commitment. In other words, because dancers work with people with whom they have a preexiting positive relationship, they are predisposed to like the people with whom they participate in dancing, and, as such, enjoy their jobs. By working with people they like and regarding their work environment as positive, they then want to continue. The acceptance and support provide positive reinforcement, thus promoting continued involvement.

Nadia's story (discussed earlier) is consistent with experiences frequently reported by dancers at social club establishments. It illustrates how the social organization of the hustle club influences dancer perceptions and adjustments and subsequent career commitment contingencies. Her work atmosphere was relatively cooperative, characterized by enduring and friendly interactions with other participants.

The club organization required her to maintain regular interaction other members of the club establishment. She was responsible for maintaining the prosperity and the cooperative atmosphere. In adjusting to the context of the social club, Nadia developed friendships and networks of mutual obligation. Because she regarded her working environment positively, she wanted to continue participating. She liked her coworkers, customers, and management and perceived her work and working environment as enjoyable. "I had to quit [due to pregnancy]. I miss Fantasy's, though. I want to still work there. I am just too outta shape, and Erik [boyfriend] really wanted me to quit. But I've seen a bunch of the guys around town. They keep asking about when I'm coming back. So I think I'll have to still work a night here and there."

Although Nadia did reduce her involvement in dancing because of pregnancy, she still continued to work on occasion. More important, her responses indicate that she did not choose to quit and wanted to continue working. Why did her career persist? Nadia's responses, like those of many of the other dancers working at social clubs, indicate that, although participation is no longer essential, continuation is encouraged through the development of personal and moral commitments. In other words, not only do dancers feel positively about the people with whom they participate in this activity, but they also feel morally obligated to them and to the establishment in general.

Although all women stated that dancing provided financial rewards, they made relatively little, but were more likely to report working when they did not have an expressed financial need. The careers of dancers in social clubs were consistently longer and characterized by more stable periods of work. One explanation behind this finding lies in the differential opportunities for commitment development. "I had to go in tonight. Anda was there practically all alone. She called and was all pissed off. She'd come in for me, so I kinda felt *obligated* [emphasis added]" (Savannah, twenty-five, danced four years).

The dancers' enforcement of informal rules regarding work attitudes and training of new dancers creates an atmosphere in which dancers have a sense of responsibility for the club. That is, they have invested in the social organization of the club. Continued participation is then essential in order maintain the social organization they have acted to create. Thus, "successful" dancers in social clubs are those who cooperate with management and fellow dancers, are sociable, and who can effectively "join" and remain in the established social network.

Amanda, who reported being in a long-term romantic relationship with a bouncer at her club, demonstrated the strength of her relationship networks: "My friend Nikki [another dancer] got me into dancing. I went to clubs with her. I hang out after work with Gabby and Tara [other dancers], get high with Phil [a customer]."

The social networks that characterize social clubs are influential in both recruiting and maintaining members into exotic dance careers. Most women reported that interest in exotic dance occurred through contact with another woman who was already dancing. This friend was influential in encouraging them to dance as well as providing suggestions and advice. This recruitment practice fosters both personal and moral commitment in that dancers both feel positively about and feel a corresponding sense of moral obligation to their fellow dancers.

Thus, the social organizational features of the social club, including symmetrical power relationships, lack of competition, network recruitment, and positive initiation and mentoring processes produce a culture that discourages hostility and promotes reciprocity norms. Adjustment to this working environment requires dancers to initiate and maintain regular, positive interactions and networks of activity. As a result, dancers in clubs like these often work because they both enjoy their jobs and want to maintain these relationships.

This socialization process provides opportunities for personal and moral commitment formation. Being actively involved in the social networks of social clubs can encourage further participation in exotic dancing in order to meet perceived obligations to other dancers, customers, or club owners. In addition to finding their jobs personally satisfying and their working conditions amicable, women reported that they felt a loyalty and sense of responsibility to other dancers with whom they were friends or a particular club or club owner.

7

CONCLUSION

I'm only being degraded if you make me feel that way.
—Sara, twenty-four, danced four years

Whether or not you should feel guilty about patronizing a strip club depends on the kind of club environment you are patronizing and how the women there experience their work. In the worlds of exotic dance, structural norms, culture, and politics create the situations in which individual action takes place and how individual actions are influenced by existing social orders. There are social circumstances in which women involved in exotic dance perceive their work as more or less degrading, more or less satisfying, and so on. To depict exotic dancing as degrading to women or as female sexual liberation oversimplifies the lives of those involved in this deviant career and ignores the larger social circumstances that surround exotic dancing careers.

But do not dancers work for the money? Of course they do. But that may not be the only reason. In fact, the relative strength of that motivation can vary substantially across social worlds. Nearly all dancers reported that they were attracted to dancing by financial benefit, excitement, and perceived ease of work. Yet, once involved, perceptions of why their participation continued was consistently related to the organizational culture and structural patterns associated with their work.[1] Regardless of the individual differences that motivate women bring to their jobs, they are subjected to variations in their work environment that impact how they think about their jobs and why they continue. For example, although two dancers may both be motivated to strip to make

money, a show club dancer may regard her work as personally satisfying and choose to continue; a hustle club dancer may only continue to work because she feels she has no choice.

In her discussion of culture in action, Swidler (1986) states:
"To adopt a code of conduct, one needs an image of the kind of
world in which one is trying to act, a sense that one can read fairly
accurately (through one's own feelings and through the response
from others) how one is doing, and a capacity to choose among
alternative lines of action" (276).

I still remember the ambivalence I felt when I ended my own
dancing career. I had long proclaimed that studies such as mine
were best done using multiple methodological approaches, and the
time came to no longer be the dancing participant observer. I
knew from the onset that dancing was only temporary. I was a
graduate student, and my real goal was to obtain my doctorate
and find gainful employment in sociology. Yet I had to face the
reality that doing research for this book had been a great excuse
to continue dancing. By taking on this project, I could minimize
the meaning of my involvement and justify being at the strip club
just a little longer. *I'm just doing research*. Right. That was simply
not true.

I had danced at clubs throughout the country, loved it and
hated it, and had had both truly wonderful and absolutely horrible experiences. And I had become obsessed with having these
experiences: my cataloging of these experiences had taken on a
meaning beyond field notes. Even now, I cannot fully articulate
what that meaning was, but I knew that I was going to miss being
in each of these social worlds, even the hustle club. Over the
years, by getting deeply involved and "backstage" in each of
these social worlds, I had seen a side of people and conditions of
daily existence that most people never see. I had seen women and
men at their best and at their worst. It was as if I got to step into
each of their lives just a little bit. Being a dancer, I had some of
the most genuine interactions with other people I had ever experienced. How ironic that these connections took place in dirty little
strip clubs.

My own firsthand experiences and the experiences of other
women suggest that how a woman perceives her work is not only
a product of intraindividual factors but is influenced by how stripping is carried out and the relative culture in which it occurs.[2]
Explaining continuity/fluctuations is asking what factors affect a

course of action, specifically, the desistance or persistence of an exotic dance career. What I put forth here is a theoretical conceptualization of the interrelationship between structural conditions and individual actions. There are organizational influences on personal enjoyment, increasing investments, and decreasing available attractive alternatives, which, in turn, explain variations in experiences of exotic dancing.

More generally, I find that the type of commitment one develops to a course of action is influenced by the social situations in which one finds oneself. Thus, independent of individual-level characteristics, whether one experiences a strong sense of personal commitment or individualized commitment to a particular task or behavior is influenced by the social structural conditions in which one is surrounded. In order for such things as personal satisfaction, feeling of obligation, and so on to exist, the social order must provide opportunities for their development.

FUTURE DIRECTIONS

Club Typology Trends

My own and other studies demonstrate that exotic dance represents both a choice and a lack of choices. The next step is to uncover factors that underlie the disparities in experiences, understand the mechanisms involved, and examine *how these conditions may be changing over time.* My experiences and observations lead me to believe that the relative presence of each social world is changing. That is, I believe that stripping is being redefined, and show clubs are becoming the dominant club typology. While I have yet to empirically assess how many of each type of club exist nationwide, my general sense, based on my years of research and dancing experiences, is that show clubs are quickly becoming the dominant club organizational style. And there is some evidence to suggest that my suspicions are correct. Rather than the low-level, small entrepreneurial endeavors such as social clubs or sleazy underregulated environments such as hustle clubs, many clubs today, such as Larry Flynt's Hustler Clubs or Rick's Cabarets, are multimillion-dollar corporations. Rick's Cabaret International, Inc., is publicly traded on NASDAQ. In a recent interview, CEO Eric Langan revealed that Rick's reported a market cap of just over

$61 million as of August 2007 (BNN, 2007). Similarly, stock prices for VCG Holding Corporation, which owns and/or manages thirteen upscale adult clubs, is up 700 percent from its initial low (Sherman 2007).

In addition, I suspect that there are differences in work outcomes related to variations in dancer mobility. Although I traveled extensively, this is a relatively less popular practice among dancers in recent years. The majority of dancers in all clubs identified themselves as "house girls" (this term refers to their practice of consistently working at one particular establishment). In contrast to the work patterns of house girls, a limited number of women, both self-identified and identified by club staff and fellow dancers as "travelers," typically only worked at a specific club for a given amount of time and then proceeded to their next location. Often, these bookings occurred cyclically, such that a dancer worked at a series of clubs over and over, working an average of one week at each establishment per booking.

My own observations suggest that show clubs discourage dancers from traveling. These clubs are motivated to keep a regular set of dancers. There are often more than enough women, and circulating the scheduling of the same dancers acts to ensure that rules are consistently followed and the dancer expectations are predictably maintained. Alternating among a steady supply of well-known dancers is compatible with a business plan of quality control.[3]

Thus, while the basics of selling "turn ons" are probably pretty much the same, the social environment in which exotic dancing occurs is changing in complex ways. The popularity of the show club and the increasing presence of sexuality in popular culture may indeed be redefining the meaning of exotic dancing and the expectations of the women who do it. My research finds that there are indeed different types of clubs and different types of occupational requirements among dancers. Trends in club organizational style across place and time undoubtedly effect variation in dancer experiences. The growing presence of the "gentlemen's" establishments (show clubs) is changing the landscape of exotic dancing.

As show clubs become dominant, how this prevailing definition of exotic dance may influence social acceptance has yet to be fully understood. While the organization of show clubs may "professionalize" these women with regard to educational opportunities and requisite commitment to dance careers, the impact of these changes with regard to social acceptance has not been explicitly examined. The changing organization of clubs and characterizations of dancers may relate to the perceptions of stigma and if stigma varies across club types. How the emergence of the professional, self-efficacious stripper and the discounting of perceptions of dancers as unintelligent, promiscuous women who cannot do anything better may bear out in interpersonal relationships is not fully known. Are show club dancers having an easier time than other club dancers with regard to experiencing and managing stigmas in their interpersonal relationships? Alternatively, the changing demographic of strippers may lead to new sources of stigmatization, as those who choose to dance may be exposed to ridicule or stereotyping from peers in their other mainstream professions.

At the organizational level, the confluence of the changing structure of dancing and the influx of the often educated and agentic women of the show club may be collectively impacting the profession with regard to health and safety. I found the world of the show club to be highly regulated. Not only were there strict rules about the appearance and conduct of dancers, but there were often highly enforced rules regarding customer conduct, such as touching or lap-dance contact as well. Other studies support my findings that these regulations may be beneficial for the health and safety of women. In an examination of club policies and health vulnerability, Maticka-Tyndale, Lewis, Clark, Zubick, and Young (1999) reported higher levels of sexually transmitted infections among dancers than estimated in the general population. They state that working in clubs with lenient touching and lap-dance policies and minimal security and surveillance increases dancers' vulnerability and customers' expectations of sexual contact. As one reporter noted, "there is no sexual contact with customers, management explains, no prostitution, no seediness like in the old-time strip clubs, and no organized crime hooks" (Sherman 2007, 1).

Thus, one positive consequence of the growing popularity of businesslike show club models of adult entertainment may be higher levels of job safety among dancers. Dancers in these establishments may differ from their counterparts in other clubs not only with regard to income but also in their vulnerability and exposure to sexual harassment or victimization.

But the show club takeover is not all good news. As show clubs begin dominating the landscaping of exotic dance, the standards for dancers may continue to increase. Thus, it stands to reason that the requisite level of commitment to the profession required increases as well. I found that show club dancers expend considerable time, energy, and money—essential for entree and success in exotic dance careers. For example, as previously noted, many women now consider plastic surgery essential in exotic dancing careers. In 2006, the average breast augmentation costs were estimated at just under four thousand dollars (American Society of Plastic Surgeons 2007). Furthermore, costs for larger implant augmentations, popular in strip clubs, are substantially higher. Many of these procedures also have significant recovery periods. Not only must dancers have the means to pay for these procedures, but they must also be financially able to survive during the following weeks, as they are not physically able to work and earn income as their bodies heal.

One must consider the possible differential impact of these changes with regard to race and class. Specifically, the increasing expectations and investment required may make this career option unavailable to some women, particularly poor women and women of color. More and more, these women, who may have relied on migratory and temporary involvement in exotic dance, are being excluded from this employment option; they lack the means to make the substantial time and financial investments required (such as gym memberships, plastic surgery, cosmetics, costumes, and hair salons).

In addition to my own findings, themes of race and class disparities in sexualized ideals are abundant in the literature (see Wesely 2003a, 2003b; Brooks 2001; Trautner 2005 for some examples). Specifically, stereotyped characteristics associated with working-class or inner-city women as well as physical attributes associated with women of color are seen as undesireable in an effort to increase the class image of dance and dancers in hustle and show clubs. Rather, the upper echelon of establishments strives to maintain a reputation for having dancers characterized as glamorous, hypermammarous, and *white*. Consistent with my work, Egan (2006a) reported that managers of Flame openly attempt to identify the club with more affluent, white (middle-class) culture. "Flame is a classy place," the owner argued, "and our customers don't want to hear rap, hip-hop, or heavy metal" (207). In contrast, she notes that the other establishment in which she worked, Glitters, is the *only remaining* lower-tier exotic dance club in a former urban red-light district. She notes that there is greater diversity in this establishment and more tolerance of differences in physical size and appearance.

These findings suggest that opportunities for dance are restricted for those who cannot attain the "high-class," white ideal. Quite simply, women of color and white women who cannot afford it are deemed unacceptable, with few exceptions. Their exclusion from the highly lucrative and managed show club relegates those who cannot attain the "Barbie Doll" image to lower-tier social club establishments. Specifically, this relegation makes dancing less profitable for both poor women and women of color. If the often entrepreneurial social clubs become run out by corporate show club competitors, these women may have fewer and less lucrative opportunities than their white or more financially advantaged counterparts.

Exotic dance, like other sexual occupations, may have historically provided a buffer for women during economic hardship. Whereas intermittent involvement in exotic dance may have provided women with limited opportunities a source of temporary income, exotic dance careers appear to be increasingly defined by diligence, constant effort, and substantial commitment. Economically challenged women may have relied on their ability to utilize this occupation, albeit at some personal, physical, or emotional cost. At a recent conference on sex work, performer and activist Jo Weldon adroitly noted, "At what other job can you start off with nothing, go in on the same day, make money all night, and pay your bills the very next day?" (Weldon 2006). The utility of sex occupations such as exotic dance at immediately alleviating financial crises must be recognized; so must the outcome of the disappearance of this option for many women. Is this opportunity becoming less available to those who may need it most? If so, what happens to these women when that opportunity is no longer viable? What are the implications of reducing the viability of this alternative? We have yet to empirically assess the impact of this potential displacement on the economic survival strategies of disadvantaged women.

Challenging the "Exploitation versus Liberation" Debate

One theme found throughout exotic dance research is the issue of personal agency versus structural constraint. Changes in the industry and the complex images of exotic dance necessitate rethinking our conceptualizations of empowerment versus exploitation and agency versus constraint. While current research frequently involves debates about the gendered nature of exotic dance and of sex work more generally (see Barton 2002; Chapkis 1997; Egan and Frank 2005; Weitzer 2000, 2005), we have yet to really tackle how trends in the industry may change the dynamics of erotic labor. Dancers today may face different challenges than their earlier counterparts, particularly with regard to financial and physical investment required to obtain hypersexualized male ideals (for more discussion see Bradley 2008).

Although many of the tips, tools, and interaction strategies persist and may be still common among all work places, *where* women strip may be more influential than the techniques of strip teasing in whether women consider their job exploitive or liberating. Club styles may foster or hinder unique stresses for women involved in stripping. What has yet to be fully understood are the structural dynamics in which dancer experiences take place. That is, although variations in club context can be clearly found across the literature, the role structural features play in the agency-versus-exploitation debate has thus far been unexamined. This book speaks to this debate by identifying the structural influences on dancer experiences and trying to unpack their meaning.[4]

As we consider issues of agency/constraint, the growing number of women working as dancers begs questions regarding women's role in their empowerment or exploitation. That is, social scientists must consider whether women's voluntary participation in exotic dance makes it any less exploitive or any less a reproduction of gender inequalities. What are popularly considered neofeminist expressions of sexuality and the changing structure of exotic dance may actually involve simply embracing hypersexualized male ideals rather than empowering women (Bradley 2008).

While exotic dancing may be empowering and/or exploitive, the stripping industry is changing. Thus, how empowerment/constraint is manifested in the course of women's work may indeed be changing as well. If erotic labor is empowering, how and why? If it is exploitative, what are the conditions that make it so? Is the experience of dancing changing, and if so, how? How (if possible) can these conditions be changed?

There are lots of possible explanations for why women enter exotic dance, just as there are a myriad of motivations behind any other occupation. Frankly, for my purposes, I do not really care. I am more concerned with the conditions of their work, how they characterize it, and why they continue to do it. By walking the reader through the worlds of exotic dance, I hoped I have demonstrated the importance of culture and social networks in explanations of sex work careers. I am not dichotomizing women working in sexual occupations as sexually liberated or as helpless victims. Rather, this study presents a conceptual framework for understanding the variability along a *continuum* of agency versus constraint, experienced both internally and externally. I find it important that the extent to which women view themselves as forced to engage in sex work is at least somewhat dependent upon the structural arrangements in which they define and experience their work. Sociologists must ask questions regarding how work is constructed and defined under particular conditions, as these conditions can vary substantially. What does it mean for them to work at an exotic dance establishment? More important, what influences the meaning of their work? In what ways does stripping embody a choice, a lack of choices, or some more ambiguous experience?

Dancers do not dance in a vacuum. Dancers work in clubs, under management, around customers and co-workers, under policies, and within formal and informal culture. Throughout these pages, my intent has been to unpack the complexity of dancing by detailing how the dancing experience is conditioned by the social environment in which it occurs. Questions regarding sexual occupations can be better informed by a perspective that incorporates such contextual variation. The social organization of the occupation creates the atmosphere in which these women work. Rather than asking if sex work is degrading or not, let us begin asking under what circumstances variations in degradation or expression, pleasure or danger, and agency or constraint are experienced.

nOTES

CHAPTER 1. INTRODUCTION

1. For some examples of workers' acknowledgment of the stigma of sex work, see Thompson and Harred (1992), Reid et al. (1994), Lerum (1998), Abbott (2000), and Thompson, Harred, and Burks (2003).
2. Many believe some classic feminist authors, such as Andrea Dworkin and Catherine MacKinnon (for example, see McKinnon and Dworkin 1989) conceptualize female sexual labor in this way.
3. See Burana (2001), Bartlett (2003), Mattson (1995).
4. These findings are not unique to exotic dance and can be found in writings by and in collaboration with a variety of sex workers. Some good examples of such include work by Queen (2003), Angell (2004), Quan (2003), Nagel (1997), and Delacoste and Alexander (1998).
5. The processual-order perspective is the dominant symbolic interactionist perspective for the study of organizational culture and social orders (Maines and Charlton 1985).
6. This systematic conceptual framework had been applied to understanding such organizational cultures and informal structures as hospital wards (Strauss 1963), the American liquor industry (Denzin 1977), and secondary school teacher organizations (Hall and Spencer-Hall 1980). Furthermore, the processual order has been applied to organizational cultures and structures related to crime and deviance, such as Farber-

man's (1975) description of the criminogenic market structure of the automobile industry and Ulmer's (1997) analysis of the dynamics of court communities.

CHAPTER 2. METHODOLOGY

1. Including such open-ended questions as "So, what's it like to work here?" "How do you feel about dancing?" or "How does it work around here?"
2. These numbers are estimates assessed at the time of writing the methodological discussion. I have truly never stopped collecting information and do not have any immediate plans to do so. Therefore, the number of and exact demographics of participants and observations is continually growing due to ongoing collection efforts.
3. Due to the emphasis on youth associated with the exotic entertainment industry, some respondents, particularly those who appeared to be older, were reluctant to disclose their age. Thus, age was sometimes estimated based on their appearance and other time-related information provided in their responses (such as the age of their children, length of career, or length of marriage).
4. The lack of future agenda may stem from the timing of my interview. Due to the provocative and intense nature of stripping before an audience, these respondents may have been intently focused on the immediate situation of their first performance. Thus, they may not have had the opportunity to reflect or make plans immediately following their first performances. To date, attempts to follow up on these respondents have been unsuccessful.

CHAPTER 3. DANCING AT THE HUSTLE CLUB

1. I recorded organization, adjustment, and commitment patterns consistent with those of hustle clubs in approximately eleven establishments during observational data collection.

CHAPTER 4. DANCING AT THE SHOW CLUB

1. I recorded organization, adjustment, and commitment patterns consistent with those of show clubs in approximately fifteen establishments during observational data collection.
2. Although the names of and specific details regarding this practice varied, the majority of show clubs observed by the author and described by interview respondents possessed a system of dancer presentation identified as characteristically similar to that of "showcasing."

CHAPTER 6. THE SOCIAL WORLDS OF EXOTIC DANCE

1. Dancers in all three club typologies reported having unsatisfactory relationships. However, the relative attractiveness of being at work rather, when compared to being at home (with significant others), is a preference reported almost exclusively by dancers at show clubs.

CHAPTER 7. CONCLUSION

1. This finding is consistent with previous deviance literature that suggests that the original causes of behavior may not be the same as later causes that entrench individuals into criminal and deviant careers (Ulmer, 2000; Steffensmeier and Ulmer, 2005).
2. In doing so, this provides empirical support for the conceptualization of continuity in deviance proposed by Ulmer (1994, 2000) and extends this conceptualization of the commitment framework by incorporating the structural precursors of the various sources of commitment.
3. Although observational data were collected on the behaviors of travelers, my findings would suggest that, by doing the same job across clubs, travelers have fewer opportunities to build the social networks that foster moral commitment in social clubs. In addition, it is possible that both show club house girls and travelers may be personally committed to dancing by the identity that dancing mobilizes. However,

because they work at a number of different clubs, travelers' personal identification with being dancers may be less related to the social organization of a particular club type. Future studies should explore the booking patterns of travelers and how potential variations in these patterns affect dancer perceptions of work and subsequent commitment contingencies.

4. Notably, recent work by Deshotels and Forsyth (2006) incorporates information from a relatively large sample of dancers and across multiple club settings. They find support for both the sexual radical/libertarian and radical feminist views regarding sex work. Importantly, this work demonstrates that club type and policies create variation in dancers' perceptions of their working environment and experiences.

SELECTED BIBLIOGRAPHY

Abbott, Sharon A. 2000. "Motivations for Pursuing an Acting Career in Pornography." In *Sex for Sale: Prostitution, Pornography, and the Sex Industry,* edited by R. Weitzer, 17–34. New York: Routledge.

American Society of Plastic Surgeons. 2007. "Average Surgeon/Physician Fees, 2006." www.plasticsurgery.org.

Anderson, Elijah. 1999. *The Code of the Street: Decency, Violence, and the Moral Life of the Inner City.* New York: Norton.

———. 2003. "Jelly's Place: An Ethnographic Memoir" (Distinguished Lecture). *Symbolic Interaction.* 26: 217–37.

Bartlett, Cheryl S. 2003. *Stripper Shoes.* Bloomington, IN: First Books.

Barton, Bernadette. 2002. "Dancing on the Mobius Strip: Challenging the Sex War Paradigm." *Gender and Society* 16: 585–602.

———. 2006. *Stripped: Inside the Lives of Exotic Dancers.* New York: New York University Press.

Becker, Howard S. 1960. "Notes on the Concept of Commitment." *American Journal of Sociology* 66:32–40.

———. 1963. Outsiders: Studies in the Sociology of Deviance. New York: Free Press.

Boles, Jacqueline, and Albeno P. Garbin. 1974. "The Strip Club and Customer–Stripper Patterns of Interaction." *Sociology and Social Research* 58: 136–144.

Bradley, Mindy S. 2007. "Girlfriends, Wives, and Strippers: Managing Stigma in Exotic Dance Careers." *Deviant Behavior* 28: 379–406.

————. 2008. "Stripping in the New Millenium: Thinking About Trends in Exotic Dance and Dancers' Lives." *Sociology Compass* 2: 503–518

Brooks, Siobhan. 2001. "Exotic Dancing and Unionizing: The Challenges of Feminist and Antiracist Organizing at the Lusty Lady Theater." In *Feminism and Antiracism*, edited by F. Twine and K. Blee, 59–70. New York: New York University Press.

Burana, Lily. 2001. *Strip City: A Stripper's Farewell Journey across America*. New York: Miramax.

Business News Network (BNN). 2007. Interview with Eric Langan. Aired August 15th. http://broadband.bnn.ca/bnn/?vid=11470.

Chapkis, Wendy. 1997. *Live Sex Acts: Women Performing Erotic Labor*. New York: Routledge.

Delacoste, Frederique, and Priscilla Alexander. 1998. *Sex Work: Writings by Women in the Sex Industry*. San Francisco: Cleiss.

Denzin, Norman. 1977. "Notes on the Criminogenic Hypothesis: A Case Study of the American Liquor Industry." *American Sociological Review.*

Deshotels, Tina, and Craig Forsyth. 2006. "Strategic Flirting and the Emotional Tab of Exotic Dancing." *Deviant Behavior* 21: 223–241.

Egan, R. Danielle. 2006a. "Resistance under the Blacklight: Exploring the Use of Music in Two Exotic Dance Clubs." *Journal of Contemporary Ethnography* 35 (2):201–209.

Egan, R. Danielle. 2006b. *Dancing for Dollars, Paying for Love: the Relationship between Exotic Dancers and Their Regulars*. New York: Palgrave.

Egan, R. Danielle, and Katherine Frank. 2005. "Attempts at a Feminist and Interdisciplinary Conversation about Strip Clubs." *Deviant Behavior* 26: 297–320.

Enck, Graves E., and James D. Preston. 1988. "Counterfeit Intimacy: A Dramaturgical Analysis of an Erotic Performance." *Deviant Behavior* 9:109–123.

Farberman, Harvey. 1975. "A Criminogenic Market Structure: The Automobile Industry." *The Sociological Quarterly* 16:438–456.

Farley, Melissa. 2004. "Bad for the Body, Bad for the Heart: Prostitution Harms Women Even If Legalized or Decriminalized." *Violence against Women* 10: 1087–1125.

Forsyth, Craig, and Tina Deshotels. 1998. "A Deviant Process: The Sojourn of the Stripper." *Sociological Spectrum* 18: 77–92.

Frank, Katherine. 2002. *G-Strings and Sympathy: Strip Club Regulars and Male Desire.* Durham, NC: Duke University Press.

Gallup poll, conducted May 28–29, 1996. Sample N=1,019.

Glaser, Barney, and Anselm Strauss. 1967. *The Discovery of Grounded Theory.* Chicago: Aldine.

Hochschild, Arlene R. 1979. "Emotion Work, Feeling Rules, and Social Structure." *American Journal of Sociology* 85: 551–575.

Johnson, Michael P. 1973. "Commitment: A Conceptual Structure and Empirical Application." *Sociological Quarterly* 14: 395–406.

———. 1991. "Commitment to Personal Relationships." In *Advances in Personal Relationships,* edited by W. H. Jones and D. W. Perlman, 117–143. London: Kingsley.

———. 1999. "Personal, Moral, and Structural Commitment to Relationships: Experiences of Choice and Constraint." In *Handbook of Interpersonal Commitment and Relationship Stability,* edited by J. M. Adams and W. H. Jones. New York: Plenum.

Lerum, Katherine. 1998. "Twelve-step Feminism Makes Sex Workers Sick: How the State and the Recovery Movement Turn Radical Women into 'Useless Citizens.'" In *Sex Work and Sex Workers,* vol. 2 in Sexuality in Culture, edited by Barry M. Dank, and Roberto Refinetti. London: Transaction.

MacKinnon, Catherine. 1989. *Toward a Feminist Theory of State.* Cambridge, MA: Harvard.

MacKinnon Catherine, and Andrea Dworkin. 1998. *In Harm's Way: The Pornography Civil Rights Hearings.* Cambridge, MA: Harvard.

Mattson, Heidi. 1995. *Ivy League Stripper.* New York: Arcade.

Maticka-Tyndale, Eleanor, Jacqueline Lewis, Jocalyn P.Clark, Jennifer Zubick, and Shelley Young. 1999. "Social and Cultural Vulnerability to Sexually-transmitted Infection: The Work of Exotic Dancers." *Canadian Journal of Public Health* 90: 19–22.

McCaghy, Charles H., and James K. Skipper. 1972. "Stripping: Anatomy of a Deviant Lifestyle." In *Lifestyles: Diversity in American Society*, edited by S. D. Feldman and G. W. Thielbar, 362–373. Boston: Little, Brown.

Nagel, Joane. 2000. "Sexualizing the Sociological: Queering and Querying the Intimate Substructure of Social Life." *The Sociological Quarterly* 41: 1–17.

Prus, Robert. C., and Irini Styllianos. 1980. *Hookers, Rounders, and Desk Clerks: The Social Organization of the Hotel Community*. Toronto: Gage.

Queen, Carol. 2003. *Real Live Nude Girl: Chronicles of Sex Positive Culture*. San Francisco: Turnaround.

Raphael, Jody, and Deborah Shapiro. 2004. "Violence in Indoor and Outdoor Prostitution Venues." *Violence against Women* 10: 126–139.

Raymond, Janice. 1995. "Prostitution Is Rape That's Paid For." *Los Angeles Times*, December 11: B6.

———. 1998. "Prostitution as Violence against Women." *Women's Studies International Forum* 21: 1–9.

Reid, Scott A., Jonathon A. Epstein, and D. E. Benson. 1994. "Role Identity in a Devalued Occupation: The Case of Female Exotic Dancers." *Sociological Focus* 27: 1–16.

Ronai, Carol Rambo, and Carolyn Ellis. 1989. "Turn-ons for Money: Interactional Strategies of the Table Dancer." *Journal of Contemporary Ethnography* 18: 271–298.

Salutin, Marilyn. 1971. "Stripper Morality." *Trans-Action* 8: 12–22.

Sherman, William. 2007. "The Naked Truth about Strip Clubs." New York Daily News. July 8. www.nydailynews.com.

Skipper, James K., and Charles H. McCaghy. 1970. "Stripteasers: The Anatomy and Career Contingencies of a Deviant Occupation." *Social Problems* 17: 391–405.

———. 1971. "Stripteasing: A Sex-oriented Occupation." In *The Sociology of Sex*, edited by J. Henslin, 275–296. New York: Appleton Century Crofts.

Smith, Dorothy. 1989. *The Everyday World as Problematic: A Feminist Sociology*. Boston: Northeastern University Press.

———. 1991. *The Conceptual Practices of Power: A Feminist Sociology of Knowledge*. Boston: Northeastern University Press.

Steffensmeier, Darrell. 1986. *The Fence: In the Shadow of Two Worlds*. Totowa, NJ: Rowman and Littlefield.

Steffensmeier, Darrell, and Jeffrey T. Ulmer. 2005. *Confessions of a Dying Thief: Understanding Criminal Careers and Criminal Enterprise.* New Brunswick, NJ: Transaction-Aldine.

Strauss, Anselm. 1984. "Social Worlds and Their Segmentation Processes." In *Studies in Symbolic Interaction* 5: 123–139.

————. 1993. *Continual Permutations of Action.* NY: de Gruyter.

Strauss, Anselm, and Juliet Corbin. 1990. *Basics of Qualitative Research: Grounded Theory Procedures and Techniques.* Newbury Park: Sage.

Strauss, Anselm L., Leonard Schatzman, Rue Bucher, Danuta Ehrlich, and Melvin Sabshin. 1963. "The Hospital and Its Negotiated Order." In *The Hospital in Modern Society,* edited by Eliot Freidson, 147–168. New York: Free Press.

Sweet, Nova, and Richard Tewksbury. 2000. "Entry, Maintenance, and Departure from a Career in the Sex Industry: Strippers' Experiences of Occupational Costs and Rewards." *Humanity and Society* 24: 136–161.

————. 2003. "'What's a Girl Like You Doing in a Place Like This?' Pathways to a Career in Stripping." In *Sexual Deviance: A Reader,* edited by C. Hensley and R. Tewksbury, 149–166. Boulder: Rienner.

Swidler, Ann. 1986. "Culture in Action: Symbols and Strategies." *American Sociological Review,* 51: 273–286.

Thompson, William E., and Jackie L. Harred. 1992. "Topless Dancers: Managing Stigma in a Deviant Occupation." *Deviant Behavior* 13: 291–311.

Thompson, William E., Jackie L. Harred, and Barbara Burks. 2003. "Managing the Stigma of Topless Dancing: A Decade Later." *Deviant Behavior* 24: 551–570.

Trautner, Mary Nell. 2005. "Doing Gender, Doing Class: The Performance of Sexuality in Exotic Dance Clubs." *Gender and Society* 19: 771–788.

Ulmer, Jeffery T. 1997. *Social Worlds of Sentencing: Court Communities Under Sentencing Guidelines.* Albany: State University of New York Press.

————. 2000. "Commitment, Deviance, and Social Control." *The Sociological Quarterly* 41: 315–336.

Weitzer, Ronald. 2000b. "Deficiencies in the Sociology of Sex Work." In *Sociology of Crime, Law, and Deviance* (vol. 2), edited by J. T. Ulmer, 259–279. Oxford, UK: Elsevier Sciences.

———. 2005a. "Flawed Theory and Method in Studies of Prostitution." *Violence against Women* 11:934–949.

———. 2005b. "The Growing Moral Panic over Prostitution and Sex Trafficking." *The Criminologist* 30(5):1–4.

———, (ed.). 2000a. *Sex for Sale: Prostitution, Pornography, and the Sex Industry.* New York: Routledge.

Weldon, Jo. 2006. "Show Me the Money: On the Absence of Financial Psychology in Studies of Sex Work." Presentation, Sex Work Matters: Beyond Divides Conference, March 30, 2006.

Wesely, Jennifer K. 2003a. "Exotic Dancing and the Negotiation of Identity: The Multiple Uses of Body Technologies." *Journal of Contemporary Ethnography* 32 (6):643–669.

———. 2003b. "'Where Am I Going to Stop?' Exotic Dancing, Fluid Body Boundaries, and Effects on Identity." *Deviant Behavior* 24:483–503.

INDEX